LITHIUM AND HEROIN

Coping with Dual Diagnosis

Phillip Graph

Illustrated by Frank Harris

AuthorHouse™
1663 Liberty Drive
Bloomington, IN 47403
www.authorhouse.com
Phone: 1 (800) 839-8640

Published by AuthorHouse 3/23/2016

ISBN: 978-1-5049-8552-9 (sc)
978-1-5049-8553-6 (e)

Library of Congress Control Number: 2016904375

Print information available on the last page.

Any people depicted in stock imagery provided by Thinkstock are models,
and such images are being used for illustrative purposes only.
Certain stock imagery © Thinkstock.

This book is printed on acid-free paper.

Because of the dynamic nature of the Internet, any web addresses or links contained in this book may have changed
since publication and may no longer be valid. The views expressed in this work are solely those of the author and do
not necessarily reflect the views of the publisher, and the publisher hereby disclaims any responsibility for them.

authorHOUSE®

About the Book

Lithium and Heroin: Coping with Dual Diagnosis is a firsthand account of one man's odyssey from mental illness and addiction. It chronicles his lifelong story struggling with anxiety and depression as a boy to schizoaffective disorder and opiate addiction as an adult. It provides insight into this dimly lit world. It recounts experiences during psychiatric hospitalizations and drug-seeking behavior with the message of hope that recovery is possible. Our society is plagued with mental illness and addiction. This story is meant to inspire others that dual diagnosis is not an insurmountable obstacle to overcome.

Introduction

I wake up flat on my back, strapped to a bed. I turn my head to the left and see my arm tied down with two metal-buckled restraints. The same is so for my right arm and legs. I think to myself, "Not even Harry Houdini could escape this predicament!"

These leather restraints have a kind of sado-masochistic air to them. They're often one of the first things you see upon admittance to a psychiatric ward. I should know. I have made over a dozen pilgrimages to these facilities over the course of my life. I don't intend on returning, but one never knows.

Do I consider myself crazy? Not really. Although without my medication, I can become psychotic and delusional. Some people who have encountered me while off my medicine probably could argue that I was insane. Perhaps the best words that describe me are "overly sensitive, too analytical, perfectionistic, and nervously irritable."

What does it mean to have a chronic mental illness so severe that you have to take life-sustaining medication the same way a diabetic relies on insulin?

Lying on my back, bound in this "seclusion room," I ask, "My God, how did I get here?"

By sharing my first-hand experiences with the reader, I hope that I can provide a beacon in this dimly lit world of mental illness and addiction.

Anxiety. Depression. Bi-Polar Disorder. Schizophrenia. Suicide. Anorexia Nervosa. Obsessive Compulsive Disorder. Addiction. Over 30% of all Americans have suffered or will suffer at one time in their lives from some sort of mental illness. It is a disease that needs to be treated like any other. But how? The mind is such an intangible part of our bodies. In the book of Jeremiah of the Bible, God says, "I knew you before you were formed in your mother's womb." This seems to indicate that our souls are timeless and immortal, however our brains are not. Mental health can be defined as the physical health of the brain. The brain is the physical repository of the soul. The soul, spirit, or mind is eternal. However, the brain like any other organ in the body eventually dies. There has to be a way of studying someone's soul or spirit. The Greeks called it "psychology," literally the study of one's spirit or "psyche." Thus, psychiatrists and psychologists probe peoples' minds in search of analyzing their behavior.

I have no medical degree in psychiatric medicine. I have no master's degree or PhD. in psychology. However, I do have copious amounts of practical knowledge about mental illness and addiction. It was earned the hard way: 16 hospitalizations, 1 near fatal overdose, and doses upon doses of psychotropic medication and narcotics. The scars that these experiences left on my soul are my diploma in human growth and development.

Dual diagnosis refers to someone who has a mental illness and self medicates with drugs and alcohol. It is sometimes called a "co-occurring disorder." As early as I can remember, I suffered from depression and anxiety. When I became a teen, I discovered that experimenting with illegal drugs seemed to make me feel better than all of the psych meds that I had ever been prescribed. Narcotics gave me a "rush," a sense of euphoria. They quieted my racing thoughts. Psych meds did nothing to make me feel happier. Rather, they supposedly controlled my thoughts and moods in order to prevent me from having manic episodes. It took many years for me to realize that narcotics, in the long run, are destructive and that being compliant with taking psychiatric medication is the best solution for staying well.

I am a believer in naturopathy. Eating healthy, exercising regularly, and taking nutritional supplements are smart ways to stay well. However, sometimes using integrative medicine is the best route to stay well. Integrative medicine refers to combining "traditional" medical techniques with more holistic approaches. "Traditional" medicine refers to allopathy -treating symptoms and not really exploring the cause of an illness. This generally means taking drugs, which can cause side effects. For example, most anti-psychotic meds cause weight gain. Yes, these medicines can control symptoms associated with mental illness, but at the cost of causing insulin resistance, where the body converts sugar into fat, instead of using it for energy. The natural, holistic model tries to treat the underlying cause of the problem. It is the naturopathic belief that no one has a Prozac or Zoloft deficiency, which is causing depression. Rather, we would try to treat the body as a whole to find out what is depressing us. Natural supplements often have "side benefits." So, that vitamin C you take to boost your immune system may also heal your gums, so that you don't suffer from gingivitis any more. Believe me, I always try to go the natural route. Drugs are dangerous. However, my psychiatrist that I've been seeing for the last 32 years always stresses to me that I have a chronic mental illness which requires medication. "You need that Zyprexa like you need oxygen," he tells me. I've tried natural supplements, detoxification, acupuncture, and massage therapy to help relax me. One example that comes to mind was when I tried the herb Kava Kava to help alleviate my anxiety. It worked really well. I felt calm and relaxed. I didn't think I needed my medication anymore. I was taking Risperdal at the time. It didn't take long before I had a manic episode, while I was still calm and relaxed on the Kava Kava.

As my doctor reminded me, manic episodes come on with me like dominoes falling. One goes down. The next thing you know, they've all fallen. A manic episode can come on like a spark and quickly turn into an inferno. I've also tried SAM-e, 5-HTP, B vitamins, St. John's Wort, and valerian. Unfortunately, I haven't felt any soothing, calming, or well being effects from them. It's a shame. Who wants to take drugs that cause unpleasant side effects? Life is not black and white. There's a lot of gray. I've found that the best way to treat my mental illness is to live a healthy life and take my allopathic medication.

Chapter One

My adult mental health diagnosis is schizoaffective disorder. This illness includes periods of mania, depression, grandiose thoughts and speech, an exaggerated sense of self-importance, feeling that one is on a "special mission," and symptoms similar to schizophrenia, such as auditory and visual hallucinations. Although I've never really heard voices or saw things that didn't exist, except when I had experimented with psychedlic drugs, I've definitely succumbed to grandiose thoughts. We all experience grandiose thoughts at one time or another. "I'm going to win the lottery." "The Pittsburgh Steelers are going to win the Super Bowl." Then, when our lucky numbers don't come in, or when the Steelers lost to the Green Bay Packers in Super Bowl XLV, we get knocked down a few pegs and have to face reality. The grandiose thoughts I'm talking about associated with my mental illness are things like cancelling my life insurance policy because I thought I was immortal and would live forever, so there would be no need for life insurance. Or thinking that I could walk out in the middle of traffic and that the cars would pass through me, since I was a "man of steel." Or thinking that I was in communication with angels and extraterrestrials disguised as human beings, who have appointed me to be on a special mission ordained by God.

I was born in Pittsburgh, Pennsylvania in 1966. I grew up in the East End of the city. I have an older sister, and my parents basically provided a supportive structure for the family to thrive. Sure, we had our family tensions and dysfunctions, but it wasn't like my Dad came home drunk and beat us up. Both of my parents worked, which enabled us to attend private schools. My sister and I received good educations and enjoyed good family memories, while growing up in an upper middle class setting.

My Dad was in the military during World War II, so he could be a "hard-ass," raising his voice and being overly critical. He did like his alcoholic beverages after coming home from work, but he never was physically abusive. He worked in a local department store, managing women's clothing. This job enabled him to travel to New York City and Europe in order to buy women's "ready to wear." We later found out that Dad was cheating on Mom. This eventually destroyed their marriage, when I was 18 and my sister was 21.

My Mom was very loving and compassionate. She had some physical ailments, namely rheumatoid arthritis and lupus. Because of these autoimmune diseases, she was on very powerful medications her whole life. In fact, when she was pregnant with both my sister and me, she was taking the steroid Prednisone and painkillers. I often wonder if both my sister's and my behavioral problems can partly be attributed to the teratogenic effects of these drugs on a fetus' brain. At any rate, Mom coped with her illness the best she could. She worked full time and was a homemaker and did a pretty admirable job.

My sister is not an easy person to get along with. She has always been combative and seems to thrive on conflict. Growing up, she had the Big Mouth and was rebellious. By the time she was 15, she had a serious alcohol problem. She kept a stash of liquor in her closet and smoked cigarettes. Despite these "growing pains," she and I usually got along pretty well: cracking jokes and laughing a lot with a fatuous and irreverent wit.

Ever since I can remember, I have suffered from anxiety and depression. As early as nursery school, I would have panic attacks and be a trembling mass of flesh, who just wanted to be with his Mama. I definitely suffered from separation anxiety. When my parents would tuck me in bed at night, I always wanted reassurance that, "Nobody is going to take me away?" In first grade, I attended a parochial Catholic school. I grew up in a Greek Orthodox home. There are some subtle but distinct differences between Orthodoxy and Catholicism. The nuns at our school did like to instill fear in the students. Sister Mary Francis warned us to be careful when walking to and from school because there was a bald-headed man who drove a sedan and would kidnap children, chop them up with an axe, and stash their body parts in garbage bags in his back seat. She also informed us that she was going to bring in a Viet Nam war veteran who had his face blown up and spends his time on one knee praying. This type of imagery just fueled my anxiety and made me a nervous wreck. There was talk at school about Limbo and Purgatory, which the Orthodox faith does not recognize. I would come home confused and asked my parents guilt-ridden questions about the destiny of unbaptized souls. My parents decided to pull me out of the Catholic school after just one year.

Growing up in the late 1960's and early 1970's, I observed the hippie generation. Obviously, I was much too young to be a hippie myself, but some of their wild hairstyles and clothing frightened me. I remember being terrified that I was going to be kidnapped by some Charles Manson Family followers. However, despite a lot of anxiety and phobias, I still enjoyed my childhood and have fond memories of family gatherings, vacations, and the Pittsburgh Steelers' Super Bowl Dynasty. Seeing Terry Bradshaw throw a 55-yard touchdown pass to Lynn Swann or watching L.C. Greenwood pummel Roger Staubach often restabilized my dopamine and serotonin levels.

I attended a private school in second grade and stayed at this school all the way until my Senior Year in high school. That first year at the Academy's Junior School was rough. More panic and just wanting to be at home. Since I was the new guy, I was the target of bullies. But coming back to third grade, I adapted well and excelled academically and socially. In fact, I was now friends with the bullies that picked on me the previous year. Now we terrorized others. Looking back on these days, I have to say that it was much better being the predator than the prey.

I tried my first beer when I was 10. My dad gave me a Lowenbrau Dark during summer vacation. I remember Elvis had died that summer of 1977.

In 1978, I was in fifth grade. I happened to catch on TV a ten-year anniversary broadcast of George Romero's "Night of the Living Dead." It was the most frightening movie I had ever seen. I thought that what I had seen in the film had actually happened. It disturbed me for months. As my mother said, it sent the message of "no hope." I was constantly looking out of the corner of my eye for zombies trying to devour me. Because this movie was shot in the Pittsburgh area, it made the threat of a Zombie Apocalypse that much more believable. The theme of this film would echo into my adulthood. Whenever I would become manic and delusional, I was convinced that the dead would come back to life and feed upon the flesh of the living. Interestingly, I was somewhat able to face my zombie demons seven years later in 1985, when I actually got to be a zombie extra in George Romero's "Day of the Dead."

When I was age 11 during a Memorial Day picnic, I tried my first cigarette. It was pretty uneventful. It was more like one puff of my great aunt's lipstick covered cigarette butt that she had discarded in the grass. It was still burning, and nobody was around to watch me salvage it out of my grandmother's back yard. My great aunt was a chain smoker. I remember her brand was Larks. She suffered from severe anxiety, depression, and mood swings. She had been hospitalized multiple times and received ECT-shock treatments. Her kitchen window-sill looked like a pharmacy – multiple bottles of prescription drugs. My great aunt had immigrated to this country from Greece at a young age. Her father (my great grandfather) was a priest who openly spoke out about the Turkish Empire. He was alerted that the Turks were coming for him to execute him. As a result, his family packed up and left the country overnight, instantly becoming refugees. Apparently, my great aunt was never the same after this life-threatening experience. I often wonder if that "fight or flight experience" can be passed down genetically to future generations. The Greeks always had to contend with invaders, whether it was the Persians 2500 years ago or more recently the Ottomans going back 200 years. I feel very strongly that my panic disorder has been inherited from countless generations whose lives were regularly in danger. This is called historical trauma.

One of the very first questions someone is asked upon admission to a psychiatric facility is, "Do you have any relatives that have mental illness?" I'm sure that every family has its share of a parent, sibling, cousin, or other close relative that suffers from mental illness and/or addiction.

Modern-day psychology and psychiatry are only about 150-years-old. Prior to that, when people suffered from behavioral or emotional problems, it was believed that they were afflicted with demons. There is the story in the book of Matthew in the Bible of the two men who were possessed by demons. Jesus drove the demons out of the men and into a herd of pigs that jumped over a precipice and drowned in the water below. We cannot discount that there may be malevolent forces or negative energies that attack us all. Some may be more susceptible than others. When someone has a gift of clairvoyance and can help the police find a missing person, they are called gifted. However, when someone hears voices to kill himself or others, they are called mentally ill. People who have schizophrenia may in fact be sensitive to other realms or dimensions of reality that most people do not perceive. I am not suggesting that all mental illness is a result of demon-possession, but negative universal forces do exist and may explain some mental illness. The true power of the Devil is that people do not believe he exists. I was recently at a mental health forum and met a talented artist who had a mental illness. He had a display of his drawings, which included graphic renditions of demons and dragons. I asked him what inspired these drawings. He told me that he sees these images. Who is to say that these demons and dragons don't exist in some realm that most of us cannot perceive?

Chapter Two

Entering sixth grade was a major transition in my life. I was hitting puberty, and I was now attending the Academy's Middle School. There was a boarding prep school feel to the Middle School. I used to walk to the Junior School, since we lived close-by. The Middle School was located in an affluent suburb, which was an exclusive, wealthy neighborhood. This meant that I had to ride a school bus. The things that happened on the Middle School bus were something out of a Charles Dickens novel. There was bullying, smoking, drinking, fist-fights, wedgies, double wedgies. Our bus driver was a hippie who played in a rock band. He didn't enforce much authority. I remember things got so bad that our Headmaster boarded our bus one morning when we arrived at school. He was furious. He directed his attention to the back of the bus, where all the eighth graders thrived. His lungs were out of his mouth, he was yelling so loud.

We were required to wear suits and ties at the Middle School. There was also a disciplinary demerit system and never ending homework. I can recall my first signs of obsessive-compulsive disorder and anorexia nervosa during this time. Gone were the days of crab soccer and battleball in the gymnasium of the Junior School, the St. Valentine's Day bake sale, and arts and crafts fairs. The Middle School demanded academic and athletic perfection. I was one of the top students in my grade, but I was compelled to exercise rigid self-control, as most people with OCD do. Those with OCD usually come in two forms: cleaners and checkers. The cleaner must wash his hands, the floor, the walls, the dishes, etc. an excessive amount of times throughout the day. Once is never enough. The obsession is a persistent, invading negative thought that the individual did not do a thorough enough job at cleaning something. The compulsion is the act of performing the cleaning ritual in order to neutralize the obsession. Checkers must check doors over and over again to make sure that they are locked and secure. A checker might have to check a stove multiple times to make sure that it is turned off in order to neutralize the terrible phobia that the house will burn down. This ritualistic behavior may have to be performed a number of times in order to certify a secure feeling. Many times this behavior is a result of superstition or irrationalism. Because I was born in 1966, I had a fear of the number 6. This was the sign of the Devil or the Beast. I felt that I was somehow influenced by the Devil. I could never perform a ritual six times because I felt something terrible would happen. I would usually perform a ritual eleven times, because that was a number of perfection to me.

Then there was my eating disorder. I had a warped perception of myself and felt that I was too fat. I would starve myself all day long and then gorge myself at dinner. Although I would never induce vomiting like a bulimic, I was constantly trying to burn calories. This was when I began long-distance running. Sometimes those that are driven to perfection will accomplish things that are truly exceptional. I completed my first 26.2-mile marathon at the age of 14. There is no doubt that starting a running regimen at such an early age strengthened my body to overcome the drug abuse in my 20's and 30's. Anorexia Nervosa and Bulimia are most often associated with young girls and women. However, both young and older men are susceptible to this disease. It all comes down to self -perception and feelings of insecurity. By rigidly controlling one's food intake, the individual feels a euphoric sense of accomplishment.

It was if I was having a middle-aged crisis at the age of 12. I became obsessed with losing weight, exercising more frequently, and excelling in my studies. I was crippled by my OCD rituals, when I would come home from school. I was picking up lint from the carpet and running up and down the steps over and over again. I felt absolute control over myself. Ironically, I was actually losing control of my sanity. That never occurred to me at that time. I felt that nobody could control me, not even the tyrants I had as teachers. While my fellow classmates were getting demerits and faltering in their studies, I was a model student. I was also increasing my cardiovascular fitness and getting leaner. However, enough was enough. I lost total perspective of what I was doing to myself. I had a pathological fear of obesity.

I was terrified to eat because I thought that I might lose control and become grotesquely flabby.

My grandmother used to tell me that the ancient Greeks had a saying: "A strong mind and a strong body." I wanted to epitomize this historic slogan. Instead I suffered from a neurotic mind and an emaciated body. I had a severe emotional problem but was unaware of this at that time. The repetitive rituals I put myself through left my home a virtual prison. I could no longer perform even the simplest task because my rituals were so time consuming. My sister felt that I was behaving this way for attention. Looking back, I think that my behavior was a form of rebellion. Instead of sneaking cigarettes and liquor the way my sister did, I would overdo things. I was suffering from a mental exhaustion from sustained panic, which stressed my body and put me into a depression. The rodent of anxiety had gnawed away at my soul. My parents decided that I needed medical intervention through the assistance of a psychiatrist and hospitalization.

Chapter Three

During the summer of 1979, I was admitted to St. Francis Hospital's children's unit. I felt apprehension as we pulled up to the East Wing of the Hospital. It was an old brick and stone building with Gothic overtones. The halls had an institutional smell. I was told to expect being institutionalized for 60 days. This was back in the day when private health insurance would pay for extended mental health hospitalizations. My peers ranged in age from 6 to 12, which was how old I was at the time. The adolescents had their own unit. They were between 13 and 20 years old. It was almost like going to summer camp. Being enmeshed with kids from different backgrounds put things into perspective for me. I realized how lucky I was to be provided for as well as I was by my parents. Some of my peers came from broken homes that were verbally and physically abusive.

Looking back at my several hospitalizations at St. Francis, I have to say that I received top-notch care there. It was an environment conducive to getting well. Sure, at the time I didn't want to be there against my will. However, the combination of doctors, social workers, nuns, staff, and patients really made a difference in my getting well.

My first day on the Children's Unit, I noticed a staff worker who had long hair and a beard. He reminded me of Jesus Christ or one of his disciples. This guy was eating honeydew melon, while I was supposed to show progress by eating pancakes and sausage. I became friends with Chris immediately. He spent a lot of time with me showing me the importance of a good diet. He was a vegetarian. This gave me insight into my eating disorder. Yes, I was anorexic and would starve myself. However, talking to Chris validated some of the denial of certain foods I didn't think were healthy, like soda pop and chips. He gave me a copy of one of Dick Gregory's vegetarian books, stressing the importance of consuming raw fruits and vegetables and nuts and seeds. On one of our outings, Chris took a couple of us to his home where he prepared watermelon juice for us from his juicer.

Over the next few weeks, my appetite did return, and I was showing improvement with my OCD. I made sure that the doctors and staff saw me eating and acting normal. We had a cookout one day in the courtyard. I asked for a second hamburger. One of the staff exclaimed, "I thought you were supposed to be anorexic!"

After one month, my doctor decided to discharge me, 30 days earlier than anticipated.

We followed up with family group therapy every week. Dr. Ruth Kane was an expert in working with children and adolescents who had eating disorders and OCD. Unfortunately, as the new school year began and I was deposited back into the family dynamic, I started to revert back to my old ways: obsessional thinking, compulsive behavior, anorexia, and overexercising. First there was the excessive brushing of teeth. Then the rug straightening and lint picking. Finally, the running up and down the stairs. My dad used to joke to relatives, "Keep him away from steps!"

I had an extreme phobia of the word "lazy." If somebody ever called me that, I felt that I wasn't working hard enough or exerting enough self-control.

The nightmare had begun all over again. I would skip breakfast, ate like a bird for lunch, and then gorged myself at supper. Before bed, I rewarded myself with bags of Pepperidge Farm cookies. Years before becoming addicted to illegal drugs, I was hooked on sugar. Refined sugar acts just like a drug on the body. It is an anti-food. Instead of providing us nourishment, it robs our bodies of nutrients. Whether it was Pepperidge Farm Molasses Crisps, Lemon Nut Crunch, or Genevas, I would get a euphoric rush after devouring these treats. Eating cookies was pretty much the one and only thing I had to look forward to during this time of my life. This was all in an effort to regain control of myself. I would deny myself nourishment all day and then overcompensate at night, after finishing my homework.

I continued to see Dr. Kane on a regular basis. During one of our family therapy sessions, Dr. Kane made the comment, "Looks like you gained a little weight, Phil!" This sent me into an immediate panic. My Dad said, "Jesus Christ, that'll set him back six months!" My parents were heartbroken because they thought that I had gotten rid of the monkey on my back. Dr. Kane told us that children often repeat their abnormal behavior when they are placed back into their domestic environment. Dr. Kane asked me if I was vomiting after I ate my only meal of the day. I said no. She mentioned the word bulimia. Nobody in our family knew what that word meant. She explained that it was an illness associated with anorexia where the individual induces vomiting after eating. In this way, the person can gorge himself and not feel guilty about getting fat because the food never gets digested. Dr. Kane said that I had bulimic tendencies. I starved myself all day and then feasted at night until my stomach hurt. Instead of throwing up, I overexercised in order to burn calories.

I was actually elated when friends and relatives told me that I looked sickly. I felt that my rigid self-control was paying off. The students at school made fun of me. They laughed at the small portions of food I ate at lunch. They laughed at the stretching and limbering exercises I did at gym. They laughed at me because I wouldn't drink soda pop or eat candy bars. One day during Health Science class, our Headmaster came in and discussed a government experiment conducted on volunteers. The subject matter was starvation. How long could a healthy grown man survive on just water? I paid close attention to this lecture. It inspired me. I thought, "Where do I sign up to become a volunteer for these experiments?"

Chapter Four

My obsessive and anorexic habits rung in a new decade: the eighties. Basically, I learned to live with my neurotic behavior. My parents threatened to put me back into St. Francis Hospital, but I guess they didn't have the heart to commit me to a mental institution again. I seemed to be able to turn my compulsive rituals on and off. Whenever there was company in our home, I acted normal. Whenever we went out to visit friends or relatives, I charmed people with my humor and precociousness. I was still a finicky eater, but most people thought that I was advanced for my age, being into running and dieting.

I suppose that the most frustrating thing about my obsessive behavior was that it seemed to manifest itself only at home, in front of my parents and sister and when I was alone. My sister felt that I acted this way in order to gain all the attention from Mom and Dad. This was probably true. However, the subconscious mind is so powerful that I had no conscious control of turning my behavior on and off. I had so much anger, guilt, and self-hatred, that I felt the need to punish myself with my rituals and dieting. The person with OCD feels an overwhelming need to overdo things through overcompensation and overkill.

I also performed well under pressure. If I had 15 minutes to catch the school bus, then I would accomplish more in 12 minutes than if I had an hour. Having a time limit enabled me to harness my racing thoughts. I could rise out of bed at 7:45 AM, straighten my sheets 11 times while simultaneously fluffing the pillows, do my limbering exercises while picking lint up off the floor, and then wipe the toilet rim while cleaning footprints from the bathroom floor. By 8:00 AM, I would be out on the street corner waiting for the school bus. I actually became euphoric while performing these rituals because I could accomplish so much in such a short period of time. There were times, though, that I missed catching the bus because I cut things so close.

On one positive note, I did become an avid runner. I ran in and completed my first 26-mile marathon in 1981 at the age of 14. Over the next 7 years, I completed 11 more marathons, including 5 New York City Marathons, The Marine Corps Marathon, and 5 Pittsburgh Marathons. People with OCD can sometimes accomplish extraordinary things, making this illness a double-edged sword.

1985 New York City Marathon. I am number 6235.

My mental illness culminated in 1983 during my Junior Year in high school. My behavior was so crippling that my parents sought the aid of a hypnotherapeutic psychologist. I enjoyed my weekly sessions with him. We talked about school and home life. The friends I had. How I got along with my family members. We covered the gamut of psychotherapy. After 3 months, I could see a look of exasperation on his face. Here was a professional who had tremendous success at helping people stop smoking, beating addictions to cocaine and losing weight. But I was an anomaly.

Dr. N. L. would try to get me into a hypnotic state and then suggest behavior modification, but there was just no change or improvement in my condition. Every session, he had me sit in an easy chair, close my eyes, and count back from 100. I would breathe deeply, thinking about each breath traveling to every corner of my body. After a few minutes, he had me visualize some place where I longed to be, such as the beach or the mountains. Then he kind of snuck up to me with a ticking clock and placed it next to my ear and said, "You will not be obsessive anymore!" This technique just didn't work. I was more concerned with making sure I didn't miss any numbers when counting back from 100. "Was the next number 54 or 53? Maybe I'll start over again from the top." Also the suggestion of carrying my breath to each part of my body made me more uptight than relaxed. "Should I visualize the breath going to each toe and finger, or are the foot and hand sufficient?" I was obsessed with how to achieve my meditative state, rather than just sliding into it.

I began to grow disillusioned with hypnotherapy. I was plagued by guilt feelings that I couldn't manage. Dr. N. L. came to the conclusion that I just couldn't control myself. Many years later, I sought the assistance of another hypnotherapist. He explained that the reason it is so difficult to control OCD and persistent negative thinking is that these thoughts originate from the deep limbic system of the brain. This part of the brain is responsible for that "fight or flight" feeling. It is almost impossible to consciously control the release of adrenaline and other hormones and neurotransmitters once the deep limbic system is aroused.

Dr. N. L. suggested that I seek the aid of a neuropsychiatrist, who could prescribe me some mood-altering medication. Dr. T. G. proposed that I had a chemical imbalance and that I needed psychotropic medication to re-establish this balance. I was also hospitalized again – this time at a hospital in the South Hills. My new doctor put me on lithium and parnate, also known as an "MAO Inhibitor." This pharmacologic protocol did not seem to help me. In fact, the parnate actually made me euphoric while I was engaged in ritualistic floor scrubbing and picking lint up off the floor of the psychiatric unit. The routine on the Unit was pretty much the same: frequent blood samples being drawn, 8 to 12 hours of television, and patients smoking.

I spent about 6 weeks at this hospital. The sad reality was that I became more and more zombified as the weeks passed by. According to the Physician's Desk Reference, "Parnate increases the concentration of epinephrine, norepinephrine, and serotonin in storage sites throughout the nervous system. In theory, this increased concentration of monoamines in the brainstem is the basis for antidepressant activity." Parnate prevents the absorption of tyramine. So, one has to abstain from foods containing this amino acid. Foods such as herring, chocolate, and cheese have to be avoided because of their high tyramine content. Otherwise, the patient can suffer from severe high blood pressure.

Some nights I'd lie in my hospital bed defiantly eating chocolate cookies. I was playing Russian Roulette, risking high blood pressure, but I needed to indulge myself in this gloomy and melancholy environment.

Lithium is used to treat mania. According to Wikipedia, "lithium ions interfere with ion transport processes that relay and amplify messages carried to the cells of the brain."

This combination of medicine made me torpid and sluggish. My father was affected by my numb listlessness. He wanted to pull me out of the hospital every time he came to visit.

Dr. T. G. really didn't bother talking to me about my feelings. He was more concerned about the side effects from the medication. He left the psychoanalysis to his wife, who was a therapist. She used "contamination therapy," which is a form of behavior modification. The nurses and staff made me touch garbage cans and then not allow me to wash my hands. Because I had an irrational, superstitious fear of the number 6, the hospital staff pasted the number 6 all over the ward – down the halls, in the TV room, and in the dining area. Other patients wondered what this was for.

I did make friends with some of the pretty nurses. I also befriended a patient, who was extremely suicidal. Dan was on 24-hour suicide watch the whole time I was there. He would pace the hall, escorted by this geriatric orderly hopelessly trying to keep up with him. His pace was like that of some caged animal. He never uttered a word to anyone until one day I offered him a handful of peanuts I carried around with me in a brown paper bag. He reached into the bag, munched on the Planter's, and said in a gruff voice, "Thanks for the peanuts."

One day the paramedics came onto our Unit with a gurney. Dan was strapped onto it and transferred into an ambulance, where he was taken to the state hospital. He was very cooperative about being tied down. However, there was still something inhumane and insensate about this. It frightened me. I never saw him again. I often wonder whatever happened to him. Little did I know that 11 years later, I would be transported to another state hospital in the same manner.

My parents were disgusted with my treatment at this local hospital. The medication was not working, and I was still hopelessly ill. Looking back at this time in my life, I wonder how a Marine Drill Instructor would have handled me. "What's the matter, Graph? Didn't you get enough love and attention from Mommy and Daddy? What is your major malfunction?" Not even motivational speaker Anthony Robbins could have snapped me out of this fugue. I was a masochist. However, I truly could not control beating myself up. I was addicted to putting myself through mental torment.

My uncle, who is a pediatrician, contacted Abraham Twerski at St. Francis Hospital. Dr. Twerski recommended that I be admitted to St. Francis' Adolescent Unit. There I was introduced to Dr. M. H. who is still my psychiatrist today after over 30 years. This was my second admission to St. Francis, during the spring of 1984. A lot of the staff remembered me from my previous admission in 1979. Dr. M. H.'s approach was a bit different from my previous doctor. He believed that I didn't necessarily need medication to be cured. He believed that interaction with other adolescents was the solution. He was heavy on Freud. According to Dr. M. H., all of my symptoms had to do with sexual energy. He asked me how many times I masturbated each day. I was a "good boy" and was looking for my reward. I learned that he used this approach with all of his adolescent patients. However, I am still trying to find the deep dynamic that propelled my insanity.

It was refreshing to be back in familiar surroundings and to be off all psychotropic medications. Being with other kids my age was therapeutic. There was swimming, games in the gymnasium, and activities in the courtyard. The courtyard was a magical place. It was an institutional oasis. The walls of St. Francis' East Building surrounded this outdoor area and provided a unique perspective to the patients. Although we knew we were confined in a mental institution, we had the freedom of being outdoors, without the risk to staff of elopement. Many a game of football, kickball, volleyball, basketball, and softball were played in the courtyard. You could sense the footprints of history left behind by the previous decades' patients. The hospital was founded in 1865 and regularly treated psychiatric patients by 1880. My level of fear was low, because I was a veteran of St. Francis Hospital. I was familiar with the environment. This can be extremely helpful for a psychiatric patient to get better. I began to realize that the therapeutic environment is a major factor in regaining one's sense of well-being. St. Francis stressed interaction with my contemporaries, physical activity, group therapy, and one-on-one counseling. The staff of nuns, counselors, and social workers was a major force that was lacking at the hospital in the South Hills. The approach there was "round 'em up like cattle, sedate them, and plop them in front of the television or in the smoking room." It's a shame that St. Francis Hospital no longer exists. The nuns reached out to all who needed help, especially those who had no health insurance. As a result, the hospital operated at a deficit until it finally closed its doors in the early 2000's.

Nowadays, there are places like Residential Treatment Facilities for youth with behavioral problems. I have visited some RTF's with the work that I do now. Most of the adolescents there that I've talked to are not happy with their treatment. They feel that the rules are too strict, that they have no freedom, and the education component is substandard. However, if a youth's behavior is so abnormal that he needs to be taken out of his domestic environment, comfort is secondary to treatment. A 14-year-old might live at an RTF for 3 months, 6 months, or even a year, depending on the severity of his behavior. Private insurance usually does not pay for the RTF. Instead, parents can apply for Medicaid for their child, even if Mom and Dad have resources and wouldn't be eligible for welfare themselves. The youth is classified as a "loophole child." Other services for loophole children include Behavioral Health Rehabilitation Services (BHRS, also known as Wraparound Services). With BHRS, a team of behavioral specialists works with a child at home and at school to make sure he stays on track and that his disruptive behavior is minimal. This can be challenging, to say the least, for the Mobile Therapist or Therapeutic Staff Support to get the child to comply. I've asked my psychiatrist if he thinks that I would have been a candidate for BHRS, had I been born 30 years later. He speculated that my behavior probably would have continued anyway and that the Behavioral Specialist Consultant would have tried to pin the blame of my illness on my parents. That being said, I have worked with many parents who truly rely and depend on BHRS to help take some of the stressful load off of them when dealing with an unruly child.

Unfortunately, as a psychiatric patient enters adulthood, sedation, confinement, and television seem to be the standard. There may be some therapy, but it is limited. Many private hospitals aren't equipped with the space to accommodate outdoor recreational activities. The mental health unit may consist of only one or two dozen beds. The hospital could be short staffed, so patients might not even be allowed to go outside to smoke. Many hospitals are smoke-free, including their grounds. Patients are given nicotine patches instead. Upon discharge from a private hospital, a mental health patient might find himself transferred to a state hospital, a personal care home, a CRR (community residential rehabilitation), or an LTSR (long-term structured residence). These facilities do provide a therapy component, however sedation and confinement are quite prevalent.

Chapter Five

Dr. M. H. discharged me from St. Francis in the spring of 1984. Going back to school and reuniting with all those friendly, happy faces boosted my spirits and made me realize that I was my own worst enemy. One afternoon, I walked into physics class and tried to blend in with the crowd. I had been absent for 6 months and then, all of a sudden, I'm wearing a lab coat and taking copious notes about steam and force. I glanced over at my good friend Adam to see him sweating profusely. He was having difficulty swallowing and was taking shallow, frequent breaths. His pal was snickering in a deriding fashion. Adam had snorted a bunch of cocaine and was tackling thermodynamics. I had heard friends discussing his self-destructive habits over the last year but had never witnessed them myself. I didn't want to believe it because it went against everything that I thought Adam and I had stood for. We had even made a pact in Fifth Grade that we would never drink or do drugs.

Well, reality hit. The reality of growing up and living life. I figured Adam was going through his own turmoil through high school. Little did I know that he was a daily drinker, a smoker of both tobacco and marijuana, and a habitual cocaine sniffer. Although Adam had been my friend since second grade, I decided to avoid him. Instead, I strengthened my friendship with Ray. After all, Ray had visited me several times at the hospital. Obviously, I didn't want my classmates to know that I was in the "nuthouse." However, I felt comfortable enough that Ray wouldn't blab his mouth at school about my nervous breakdown.

Ray and I both liked filmmaking, "Star Trek," and scriptwriting. During the summer of 1984, we filmed a Star Trek spoof in his basement. Ray played Captain Kirk, and I portrayed Dr. McCoy. This project helped me get my mind off of my OCD. The reality of how difficult motion picture production is quickly sank in on us. Guys were going on vacation two weeks into the shoot. All of a sudden, the actor that played Mr. Sulu was different. Spock's ears kept falling off. There's a big difference between latex and Play Dough. The guy that played Mr. Chekhov got into a car wreck that claimed his two front teeth. We had worked Eric so hard that he fell asleep at the wheel going home one morning. Eric had helped us build the set, pick up actors, and get food. I don't know if Starfleet had a comprehensive dental plan, but Ray and I sure didn't. A worried mother called Ray's house looking for her son who was playing Scotty. We explained, "Your son is ten parsecs away from Earth in the gamma quadrant. He won't be home for dinner."

By August, tempers were really flaring. Instead of being like George Lucas and Steven Speilberg, Ray and I were more like Hitler and Mussolini. We argued over lighting, camera angles, directing, and so on. Each of us wanted to make sure that we had creative control over the project. The tension culminated when Scotty left his post because his father needed him to come home and mow the lawn.

We lit several smoke bombs in Ray's basement to portray the damage to the Enterprise. This destroyed any vestiges of cohesion among the crew. The actors were overcome by smoke inhalation. Everyone abandoned ship except Kirk. This wasn't supposed to happen. Ray adlibbed and took control of the helm. I still remember seeing this pudgy figure hunched over the ship's controls. The thick cloud of smoke exaggerated Ray's paunch hanging over his Starfleet-issue belt buckle. The climax of the scene occurred when Ray split his pants while incurring a photon torpedo. His mother came down from the kitchen, walked onto the bridge, and put an end to our space adventure.

During this time, my mother informed me that Dad was seeing another woman. This shocked me. I couldn't believe it. I became even more uncomfortable when I was around my father. Years later, my mother and I speculated that perhaps some of my abnormal behavior was due to the dysfunction between Mom and Dad. Dad had admitted that throughout their marriage, he was unfaithful. I suppose the temptation was too great for him working in a department store where he traveled with models. Perhaps my mental illness was a reflection of his deceitful lifestyle.

I decided that I should buckle down for my Senior Year of high school. I still had a shot of graduating on time with my class, even though I had lost the majority of my Junior Year. My mental illness made me falsely believe that all I had to do was apply myself. Get focused. Then I could defeat my repetitive, ritualistic behavior. The reality was that my OCD was crippling. I was realizing that one just doesn't "snap themselves out" of a disturbed state of consciousness. My father shoving Keebler Elf snack crackers into my mouth didn't cure me of my anorexia nervosa. When he told me, "The day you eat a hot dog is the day I know you're normal" did little to change my eating habits. I sort of came to terms with my demons and made gradual progress, as I matured through adolescence. This took several years. The obsessions and compulsions were like the barnacles on the keel of a ship. One might be able to eradicate most of them, but a few still remained, stubbornly clinging to my psyche.

My high school counselors suggested to me that I coast through my academics and not get bogged down with extracurricular activities. Strive for B's and C's and make it to graduation. No cross country, no yearbook, no filmmaking. I didn't want to give just half an effort. I had to try my hardest. The perfectionist in me would not allow me to relax and settle for mediocrity. I was no longer with my advanced placement chums that I had studied with since Sixth Grade. Every afternoon, I would see the cross country team doing wind sprints on the lacrosse field. I felt ashamed of myself, as if I was living in a state of ignominy.

By late October, my mind began to wander. The underlying depression which fueled my OCD began to convince me that I was worthless. I was without honor. Nobody in that high school cared one way or another what classes I was taking or what sports I didn't participate in. The pressure came from within me. My unrealistic standards of hyperperfection were grounded in fear, insecurity, self-doubt, and self-hatred.

I stopped attending classes and redirected my energy to the audiovisual club. Ray and I reconciled. We decided to take a road trip to California and create our own destinies in Hollywood. We got as far as St. Louis, when we ran out of money. Luckily, Ray had a sister there. Her family provided us with food and lodging for a few days. We contacted our parents who urged us to come home and finish school. Upon returning to Pittsburgh, Ray told his parents that I was the mastermind of the road trip. They called my parents and told them that I was a bad influence on their son.

I felt betrayed by Ray for pinning the blame on me. I thought that he and I were best friends. However, the reality of Mommy and Daddy taking away his sports car and allowance superseded any friendship we had.

Meanwhile, the dean of students informed me that I was running out of chances to graduate on time with my class. He began talking about summer school as the only way to compensate for my poor attendance. I decided to stop loafing with Ray. We stopped talking to each other, and I started hanging out with my old pal Adam. I told him about my predicament.

He gave me a kind of pep talk. He said that I was one of the smartest guys in the school and it would be a damn shame to see me get thrown out or delayed while all these half-wits would be graduating on time.

He then suggested that I party down with him one day after school. He said that I would be turned on to a new world, a new reality that would help me graduate. I was hesitant at first, but I was desperate to shake this anxiety and depression. Adam said, "Dude, snort some lines, and you'll be cool." So, one day after school Adam approached me while I was waiting for the bus. He flashed me a pack of Marlboro cigarettes and said, "I'll give you a ride home."

After we drove off campus, Adam proceeded to open up his crush-proof box of Marlboros. He grabbed a cigarette, but he also peeled back the silver wrapping around the smokes to reveal a secret compartment. From there he pulled out a rectangular package. "The answer lies in here," he said. He suggested that we go to his house "to listen to some records" in his bedroom. We got to his house, said hello to his mother in the kitchen, and went upstairs to his bedroom. Adam shut the door, put on a Joe Jackson album, and took the mirror off the wall and put it on a table.

From his desk, he pulled out his "tools" of paraphernalia. There was a steel razor blade, several glass straws, some Windex, and paper towels. He laid the mirror down on the table, gave it a few squirts of Windex, and meticulously cleaned every square inch, including those hard to get corners. I remember obsessing over how carefully he had cleaned the mirror and if I could do as thorough of a job.

Adam pulled out the rectangular package from his Marlboro Reds and carefully opened it up to reveal a white powder. It was not uniformly sifted. Some of it was in chunks, as one would find in a container of grated Romano cheese. The substance had a crystalline sparkle to it. It was cocaine.

He dumped it on the mirror and began to chop it up with his razor blade. After about 5 minutes, he started forming lines out of this pile of powder. He formed a letter "A" for himself and a letter "P" for me. I had never seen my good friend of ten years so enamored by anything. Adam bent over the mirror and aardvarked his initial "A." He handed me the straw and said, "You would have to be subhuman not to enjoy this." I snorted my letter "P" in two spurts. Within a few minutes, I noticed that my sinus cavity and front teeth were growing pleasantly numb. The palms of my hands began to sweat. My heart started pounding. All of a sudden, I had an epiphany. I was euphoric. I had this overwhelming sense of confidence and well-being. The need to perform compulsive rituals was gone. There was no obsessional thinking. I had this sudden realization that I had nothing to worry about in life. All was well.

My existence was joyful. I even called my psychiatrist and told him that I was cured. I had everything worked out, or so I thought. We continued to party that afternoon, but by the time Adam drove me home, my epiphanic elation started disintegrating. After the cocaine started wearing off, I began to feel let down and depressed. My world started crashing in on me. It was if I had been flying in the air and suddenly my wings were clipped. Now I was beginning to experience a profound anxiety attack. The dopamine and serotonin receptors in my brain, first overloaded, were now depleted. I had my first experience with "coming down" from a high. There are some theories that the word dope comes from dopamine, because dope makes you release the feel-good chemical dopamine.

It is interesting to note that patients with depression are sometimes prescribed amphetamine stimulants to kick start their brains into an elevated state of well-being. I caught a glimpse of this by self-medicating with cocaine. Also, children with ADD and ADHD are often prescribed amphetamine substances such as Ritalin and Adderal to paradoxically stimulate their autonomic nervous systems to slow down. Again, I wonder if I had been born 20 or 30 year later, would I have been diagnosed with autism or ADD, since my OCD behavior often mimicked the symptoms of these diseases. Whether it's cocaine or Ritalin, I do not sanction giving anyone, regardless of their age, a stimulant which can lead to addiction and damage the brain, heart, liver, kidneys, and nervous system.

One time after a cocaine binge, Adam was about to drive me home, when I told him to leave me up by Pitt Stadium. I wanted to run home, which was about five miles away. This was before athlete Len Bias died of a cocaine overdose during a basketball game. I can relate to what he must have felt like. I wanted to enhance my athletic spirit. I wanted to achieve a feeling of glory. This feeling was lacking in my life.

After about 15 minutes of running, I started getting the feeling as if I wanted to choke and was gasping for air. I started to lose my balance and fell into the street. I had tried to jump up the curb and missed. I severely skinned my knee. I resumed running and did make it home. My heart was pounding at 194 beats per minute. After several minutes my pulse decreased to 170, then 120, then to 90 until the coke wore off.

I tried cocaine a few more times but now anticipated the let-down or crash, after it wore off. Adam suggested that I drink alcohol to stave off that feeling or procure more coke. I tried to do that, but did not really enjoy it.

The reason that cocaine makes you feel good is because it is a triple reuptake inhibitor. This means that the neurochemicals serotonin, norepinephtine, and dopamine linger across brain synapses at the neuroreceptor sites longer than normal. Normally, neurotransmitters will recycle or "reuptake" neurochemicals like serotonin after they have crossed the brain synapse. By inhibiting this reuptake, an enhanced sense of well-being occurs. Some anti-depressants work in the same way. SSRI's (selective serotonin reuptake inhibitors) like Celexa keep serotonin longer at the neuroreceptor sites, before it is recycled or "reuptaken" by the neurotransmitter.

Chapter Six

I continued to skip school and was finally asked to leave. I took the G.E.D. test in the late fall of 1984. I passed with flying colors. The vocational school that administered the test informed me that I got the highest score ever recorded in Western Pennsylvania. I enrolled at the local university in January of 1985. Ironically, after all the trials and tribulations in high school, I was the first in my class to attend college.

I got a job as a busboy at a restaurant. The kitchen crew called me "Spunky," because of all my enthusiastic energy. You can imagine the kind of job I did as a busboy with OCD. The tables, silverware, glasses, and seats were never so clean.

I took filmmaking classes and had the opportunity to be a zombie extra in George Romero's "Day of the Dead." It was cathartic to face my fears and meet the director who had scared me so seven years earlier, when I saw "Night of the Living Dead" for the first time.

**On the set of '"Day of the Dead." January 1985.
Makeup by Tom Savini and Greg Funk.**

Because Dad's finances weren't the best, we had to sell our house. Mom filed for divorce. She and I moved in with her mother, while Dad lived with his mistress, whom he eventually married. My sister was away at college, but when she came home for holidays, she directed all of her anger at Dad. She felt betrayed by his actions toward Mom. My sister experimented with drugs and continued to drink while away at school. I visited her several times at college in New York. We had good times. I enjoyed myself hanging out with the older crowd. By graduation, my sister had abandoned the partying lifestyle and got a job with a computer company in California.

During the summer of 1985, Adam turned me on to marijuana. It's easy to snort cocaine at home, but smoking pot creates a profound odor. As a result, we had to "toke" on the road and in parks. I wasn't big on smoking things, since I was a runner. When I would smoke, he kept urging me to "Inhale! Inhale!" Finally I got the high. I remember thinking that I was in my own unique world. The marijuana we smoked was fresh and potent. I remember one July evening sitting on the hood of Adam's car in the park. The trees were so lush with their saturated green leaves. Even in the obscure, shadowy night they were quite radiant. I remember the music from the car's tape player was cranking and my mind, my soul was at peace. Gazing at the trees, I noticed that the face of an old wise man gradually appeared.

I can recall feeling very hungover, almost like in a brain fog the next day. But I enjoyed it so much that eventually that next day fog diminished as my tolerance increased. Reefer enhanced my senses. Colors were more vivid. Music was more intense. It knocked out that part of my brain that was always so hyperactive. The racing thoughts, hypervigilance, uneasiness, and nervous irritability were subdued.

"The main active chemical in marijuana is delta-9-tetrahydrocannabinol, otherwise known as THC. When pot is smoked, THC quickly passes from the lungs into the bloodstream, which carries the chemical to the brain and other organs. THC acts upon specific areas in the brain, called cannabinoid receptors. This sets off a series of cellular reactions that lead to the 'high' that users experience. Some brain sites have many cannabinoid receptors, while other areas have few or none. The highest density of cannabinoid receptors are found in parts of the brain that influence pleasure, memory, thinking, concentrating, sensory and time perception, and coordinated movement. (www.drugabuse.gov/publications/drugfacts/marijuana)

For me marijuana opened up doors of insight that I normally wouldn't have discovered, especially since my soul was trapped in this thought/mood disorder. It calmed my phobic, chaotic mind. There were times when it exaggerated my OCD. It could drive my thought mechanism into a labyrinth of racing thoughts. Sometimes it greatly increased my hypervigilance. However, the more I smoked, the more I was able to harness its therapeutic powers.

I began realizing that I had this underlying anger, which masqueraded itself as OCD. It was the kind of rage that befell a Tyrannosaurus Rex during the Ice Age. That last tropical night turning into freezing agony. Those terrible lizards must have let out some blood curdling screams during their last hours on Earth.

As I smoked my way into psychoanalysis, I realized that I just couldn't let go of whatever was bothering me. Anger is anger, but what is causing it to be so profound? Why has my subconscious mind turned this rage into a thought/mood disorder? We all have beasts buried deep within. Why does the monkey on my back have such a stranglehold on me? Sometimes people who are crazy are referred to as being "mad." Is it any wonder, then that mental instability has to do with anger or "madness?"

I pondered the concept of reincarnation. I had read and seen programs on television that connected one's issues of the present to past lives. I always felt that I had the mindset of a slave or a prisoner or a battle-fatigued soldier. I find it quite plausible that an individual could carry the burdens or unfulfilled karma of past lives into his or her present incarnation. I had met an individual who was gifted with clairvoyance. The first time I met him, he gave me specific details of some of my past lives. He told me that I was killed in the third year of the Trojan War, that an arrow had pierced me in the throat. I had been an artist who died at a young age from a plague. I served in the Roman Army and was told to carry out an order that would have certainly met my death. I deserted instead and was put on a proscription list, where I was apprehended and died in the coliseum. These conversations I had with this psychic were well before movies like "Troy" and "Gladiator" were released. Whether or not any of this information is true, I don't know. But it does explain and gives insight into why my mind is constantly on guard, why I feel that I have to overexplain myself to people in authority, and why I have dedicated this life into bolstering my health and immune system with proper nutrition. It also sheds some light on the rigidity of my military-type thinking. I don't believe that we are meant or supposed to contemplate past lives in our current life, if reincarnation is really even a law of the universe. However, it does provide insight into our present behaviors.

Trojan War Veteran

It was therapeutic at first to excogitate over these metaphysical issues. However, marijuana, as with most psychoactive drugs, stimulates the pleasure centers of the brain, which quickly become accustomed to this high. What was once just a weekly escape started becoming a daily habit. Self-medicating an already unstable mind ultimately creates an even greater imbalance, even though the drug temporarily alleviates the pain. Moderation was something I had to learn. When first smoking marijuana, the user feels that his senses are enhanced, but chronic use actually dulls the senses and makes the user feel numb and without ambition.

My mother and I were now living with my 78-year old grandmother. I used to sneak into her basement at night, open up the cellar door, and toke up. I'd come up the stairs, and my grandmother would be waiting for me. She never yelled at or scolded me. We would just sit in the kitchen and have pleasant conversations. I guess I didn't realize how pungent the odor of marijuana could be. Besides, grandmothers know everything that their grandchildren are up to.

Chapter Seven

After working as a busboy at the restaurant, I got a job at a motion picture laboratory. I was the courier/messenger for the lab. I delivered and picked up videotapes and films from various clients all over the city. This enabled me to establish contacts for freelance production work. One of the more memorable experiences was working as a camera assistant for Michael Jackson concert films in 1988 during his "Bad" Tour.

In the Spring of 1987, my friend Adam got sober. His cocaine habit had gotten so much out of control that he checked himself into Rehab for a month. He became very enthusiastic with Alcoholics and Narcotics Anonymous. The guy that had turned me onto marijuana and cocaine now encouraged me to attend AA and NA meetings with him. I went to a few meetings with him, but I never had the desire to abstain from my partying ways. I knew that Adam had a serious substance abuse problem, whereas I felt that I was a recreational drug user. You have to hit rock bottom with addiction before you are willing to change your ways. I had not reached that point yet.

I moved into my own apartment in the fall of 1987, just shy of my 21st birthday. I continued to major in Film Studies, as well as taking film production classes. My emotions were pretty stable, and the OCD had diminished. Living alone at that young age helped me "get to know myself." My mother insisted that the reason my behavior improved was because I was "out of the company of that SOB (my father)." I have read accounts that adolescents with crippling OCD tend to improve when they leave the environment that they grew up in.

My mother remarried in 1988 to someone who was 23 years her senior. Michael was more like a stepgrandfather to me and my sister than a stepfather. He was a very kind and gentle man. He took care of my mother and was able to provide emotional and financial security - things that my father could not toward the end of their marriage. In 1989, my Dad married his mistress or as my mother called her, the "bimbo." He was 26 years older than she.

It was always a challenge during the holidays for me and my sister to split our time visiting with Mom and Dad. It felt like being with Mom and her family was the norm, while visiting Dad and our stepmother was forced and unnatural. I got along in both environments. However, the tension between my sister and stepmother was extreme.

By the time I turned 21, I started going to bars on weekends with friends. I had my own apartment in a trendy neighborhood, so it was pretty convenient to walk up the street and hit some clubs, hear some jazz, drink 6 Rolling Rock beers, smoke a joint, and not have to worry about having to drive home. All that I would have to do is stagger back to my apartment. I enjoyed catching a good buzz with beer and pot. I wasn't into hard liquor. No mixed drinks. I was a drinker on weekends and a daily pot smoker.

In late 1988, I went into business with two brothers I had known from high school. Their father, who had recently passed away, was a wholesaler of color televisions and stereo systems. The brothers' idea was to get into video production. They asked me if I would be interested in becoming the production manager of this kind of business. I jumped at the opportunity. This meant a steady paycheck in the work that I loved. No more feast or famine with the freelance lifestyle, while supplementing my income working in restaurants.

Over the next two years, we built up a pretty successful business. This was way before the days when consumers could edit video on their home computers. Video enthusiasts would come to us to rent high-end video cameras and use our editing facilities.

At this time, I also reconnected with a friend who was 11 years older than me. I originally met him in 1980 when he dated one of my sister's friends. Les was a musician. In fact, he scored the musical soundtrack for my first 16 mm short film in 1986. I would occasionally see him in bars, but we really didn't start socializing or, I should say, partying until 1989. I was 23 and he was 34. Les would tell me stories about the good old days in the late 1960's and early 1970's, when artists were genuine and people weren't so interested in the me decade of the 1980's. I looked up to him like a big brother.

He also introduced me to the world of opiates. Percocet, Vicodin, Dilaudid, Hycodan, Tussionex, heroin. Downers like Valium, Ativan, and Quaaludes. Drugs that I had never heard of like "Dors and Fours," also known as Sets or Loads.

By 1990, I was accentuating my daily pot smoking with taking pills now on weekends. I stopped drinking beer on weekends and replaced it with opiates. Les introduced me to a guy that sold all kinds of pills. His name was Seth. Seth was a Viet Nam veteran. At first I started out by maybe taking 2 or 3 Vicodin painkiller tablets on a Friday night or 3 or 4 Hycodan cough suppressant tablets. I truly enjoyed the rush of opiates more than the barbaric buzz of alcohol. Opiates were cleaner and more euphoria producing. When combined with marijuana, opiates created a high that I really cherished. They stimulated my creativity. They also seemed to fill a void that couldn't be satisfied with alcohol. I could be high on opiates but still function relatively well versus the intoxicating and paralyzing effects of alcohol. Opiates also helped to control my obsessive/compulsive disorder, phobias, and anxiety better than beer.

The body has two types of nervous systems: the sympathetic and the parasympathetic. Sympathetic refers to "fight and flight." Parasympathetic refers to "rest and heal." Someone with anxiety and OCD has an overly active sympathetic nervous system. When I would take opiates, they would calm my sympathetic and stimulate my parasympathetic nervous system. Conversely, students, truck drivers, soldiers in combat situations, and people who need to stay alert commonly abuse caffeine, cocaine, and methamphetamines to stimulate their sympathetic and subdue their parasympathetic nervous systems.

Then there were the Dors and Fours or Sets and Loads, as we would call them. Dors and 4's were a combination of the sleep medication Doriden (aka Glutethimide) and Tylenol 4 with codeine. The synergistic effect of combining a hypnotic with an opiate created a synthetic-like heroin. After taking a set, the user would feel an orgasmic rush within 30 or 40 minutes. Words cannot describe how incredible this rush was, except that you could be a homeless person living in a dumpster and still feel wonderful. After this initial rush, the user would feel a narcotic suppression that would require you to lie down or nod out for the next 8 to 12 hours. Dors and 4's were very dangerous. They were extremely habit-forming and toxic. Not only did the body form a dependence on the codeine, but the user became increasingly addicted to the Doriden. Les and Seth took a set every day. I was somewhat more conservative and limited their use to twice per week. It took 3 or 4 days to recover from taking a set, so by the time I was feeling more emotionally and physically stable, I would pollute my body again with another set. I became obsessed with that initial rush, while conveniently ignoring the following 12 hours of narcotic suppression and 2 days of constipation. After the rush wore off, if you tried to stay active and move around, you would most likely end up with nausea and a severe headache. I can recall taking a set on a Friday night, walking up the street to a local resaurant, ordering dinner, and waiting to feel the rush. Then after about an hour or so, I would make a bee-line to the couch in my apartment and be knocked out for the rest of the weekend. Sets were all about chasing the rush, feeling extremely sociable for half an hour, and then managing the suppressed narcotic stupor that followed. If you never experienced symptoms associated with bi-polar mental illness, abuse Dors and 4's for a couple weeks. Then you'll know. After your body got used to the sets, the withdrawal from them was a nightmare. Not only is your body accustomed to the Tylenol with codeine, but you also become physically dependent on the Doriden and the synergistic compound it creates with the Tylenol 4.

One time I mixed cocaine with sets. Because of my predisposition toward anxiety, I was never that enthusiastic about getting high from cocaine. One evening I ran into an acquaintance at a bar. He told me that if I was ever interested in cocaine, he would give me a really good deal for $300. I took him up on that offer. The first mistake I made was snorting the coke without a "parachute." In other words not having a downer or sedative to take the edge off the coke, since it is such a powerful stimulant. Plus this coke was cut with speed or something that really intensified my anxiety. By 2:00 AM, my heart was racing and all I could think was, "You're going to have a heart attack any second." Somehow I managed to fall asleep and swore I would never do that again. I didn't want to flush the coke down the toilet, so I just saved it "for a rainy day."

One evening after purchasing a set from Seth, I thought, "What if I take this load as a foundation for relaxation and then see what happens when I snort some coke?" It was kind of like a speedball. Although a true speedball is when someone injects cocaine and heroin at the same time. I noticed that I was sedated enough on the load that when the coke kicked in, it was a pleasant euphoria without that speedy edge. This was a very dangerous experiment, abusing a downer and upper simultaneously.

I remember trying to stop taking sets. Coming off of them was pure hell. The muscle twitching, the paralyzing headaches, the inability to sleep, the skin lesions. I had never experienced auditory hallucinations before, as many schizophrenics do. When I was withdrawing from sets, I heard voices, especially at night when I tried to sleep. Les and Seth told me that it took 6 months before they could sleep normally, after stopping Dors and 4's.

My friend Gary described his set experience quite succinctly. "I went up like the Challenger." In other words, the first few moments were glorious, and then he exploded liked the doomed space shuttle. Gary told me he had to take Dramamine the following day to control his motion sickness from the set.

Then there was Tussionex. That same year, 1990, I ran into another classmate from high school. I had heard that he had a real drug problem, so it was no surprise to me when he asked me if I wanted to meet a doctor who would prescribe me Tussionex. I didn't even know what that was. He just said, "It'll get you high!" I was game. So, one morning I went with Ron to see an ear, nose, and throat doctor. He waited in the car and coached me on how to get over on the doctor. "Just tell him you have a cough and that you need Tussionex." I went in, saw this elderly physician, and came out with a prescription for 4 ounces of Tussionex. Tussionex is a narcotic oral suspension cough suppressant made from hydrocodone polistirex. The recommended dose is one teaspoon every 12 hours. Well, when I got the prescription filled, Ron split the 4-ounce bottle with me. He told me to swig the remaining 2 ounces all at once, 12 times the prescribed dosage. Needless to say, I got really buzzed. In fact, after smoking some pot with the Tussionex, I would shut my eyes and see Walt Disney-type hallucinations. This experience with the Tussionex also introduced me to a world with which I was not familiar – doctor shopping. You find a doctor who is known as a "writer." You see him maybe once per month and you get prescriptions for narcotics.

1990 was a pivotal year regarding my mental health and substance abuse. I had quit my job as the video production manager and dedicated my life to getting high. I can't honestly say that I was using narcotics exclusively to try to escape my bouts with OCD and anxiety in as much as it just felt really good. At the age of 23, I was in the experimental artist stage in my life.

I had the ponytail and was now following the Grateful Dead up and down the East Coast. I experimented with LSD, as well. I enjoyed LSD. I never really had a bad trip. In my opinion, the LSD experience was similar to smoking some really strong marijuana with plenty of visual hallucinations, laughter, and intense emotions. Some of my friends or fellow Deadheads would take acid every day when they attended concerts. They told me that the body builds up a tolerance to the LSD, so you have to take more and more after each day. I never did this. Because of my bouts with mental illness, I did not want to overdose on a psychedelic and have a "bad trip." I would say that I've taken LSD maybe 8 to 10 times in my life.

It's ironic that people tripping on psychedelics look forward to and anticipate hallucinations or cross-wiring of the senses. Tasting colors. Smelling sounds. While schizophrenics will do anything to rid themselves of hallucinations, even taking anti-psychotic medications to subdue these voices and visions.

By 1991, I was continuing to smoke pot every day and abusing opiates at least 3 to 4 times per week. I now started experiencing physical dependence on opiates. If my system didn't have opiates, the mental and physical cravings were extreme. I was obsessed with the "crush of the opiate rush." Without them, I felt depressed and experienced chills and headaches. It was also difficult to sleep. I was back at work delivering sandwiches near the university campus. Ron, the former classmate that turned me onto Tussionex, introduced me to Shawn. Shawn lived with his mother and dealt pills out of their apartment. He talked like a gangster. "Yea, Phil, dis is Shawn, OK. I've got ES's for $8.00 apiece and Valiums for $5.00. OK. OK. So what are you gonna do?" It wasn't long before I was doing business with Shawn several times per week. One day he turned me onto stamp bags. Stamp bags contain a white powder - a synthetic form of heroin that can be snorted, smoked, or injected. Stamp bag powder is usually made from fentanyl – a narcotic analgesic used for surgery. I snorted 2 lines of this white powder and enjoyed it. The rush was almost instantaneous, usually felt within minutes. I liked stamp bags better than pills because I didn't have to wait 45 minutes before feeling the drug's effects. Shawn would say, "Yea, Phil, if you go to the projects with me, I'll knock $5.00 off per bag." One time I was stupid enough to take my car and drive Shawn to the projects to procure stamp bags. All of a sudden, I was his best friend. "OK, buddy, OK, let's drive to New York and get the Merenguez. We'll tape it to the bumper. We'll never get caught!" Stamp bags would have various illustrations on the wax part of the bag, so that addicts can easily identify a good batch from a dealer. Logos such as "Murder, Inc.," "D.O.A.," "China White," and "The Beast." Shawn was particularly fond of the Merenguez – named after some Latin American island. One evening I had just guzzled some Tussionex. Shawn called me and convinced me to buy 2 stamp bags from him. When

I got them, he encouraged me to snort a bag in front of him. I told him that I had already taken some cough syrup. "Buddy, OK, I want to see you get off! I want to see your eyes get pinned!" Like a moron, I snorted the bag. I remember waking up later that night with rapid heart beat and shallow breathing. Opiates suppress respiration. In a large enough quantity, opiates will arrest respiration. I remember being so freaked out by this, that I flushed the contents of the remaining stamp bag down the toilet. Unfortunately, this experience didn't scare me enough to stop using heroin altogether. That would take another 8 years.

By the summer of 1991, I began experiencing psychotic thinking. At the time I did not recognize my thoughts as being psychotic, as a result of a "substance-induced psychosis." I started believing that I was Jesus Christ. In hindsight, maybe my subconscious mind was reaching out to a Higher Power like Jesus Christ to release me from my addictive behavior. At any rate, this grandiose and psychotic thinking culminated when I was found naked outside this woman's apartment, whom I was quite fond of. Needless to say, this stunt didn't win her affection, but it did wind me up at a psychiatric clinic courtesy of the Pittsburgh Police. I was an inpatient there for about 7 weeks. During this time, I did a lot of soul searching, however, my mind was not quite right. I was convinced that this hospital was actually a space ship. I believed that there were angels disguised as humans working at the clinic and that it was close to the apocalypse. I believed that I was really being kept there because I was chosen to help repopulate the Earth after its impending doom. I wanted to donate my heart to be used as a fuel pump for the space ship I thought I was on. The doctors put me on Trilifon - an antipsychotic medication, and lithium – a mood stabilizer. The medication made me gain 30 pounds. This was my first experience with the unpleasant side effect of rapid weight gain caused by psychotropic medication. Although, most people told me that I looked healthy. One person told me that I looked "well-rested." I was discharged in early October.

I briefly lived with my mother who was now remarried and living in a town about 40 miles southeast of Pittsburgh. Ultimately, though, I wanted to live on my own. What 24 year-old young man who likes to party wants to live with his mother? My friend Adam who was now in AA encouraged me to attend meetings and stay sober. I didn't want any part of this. I got my own apartment back in Pittsburgh and stopped taking my psychiatric medication. I was inspired by the Jay the Juiceman infommercial I had seen on TV. I started juicing organic fruits and vegetables and got back into running. I was able to lose most of the weight I had gained while at the psychiatric clinic. However, I still liked to party. In fact, now I would smoke marijuana before going out to run. I liked to get high and go out and run 4 or 5 miles while listening to the Grateful Dead on my sports Walkman. And I still abused opiates. Looking back on this period of my life, I'm amazed at how I abused myself but still maintained or tried to maintain a healthy lifestyle by eating healthy and exercising regularly. This type of fast living, burning the candle at both ends, lent itself to the mindset of the bi-polar or manic thought process – one extreme to the other. I was now 25 years old.

By the summer of 1992 I moved to a suburb outside of Pittsburgh. Nothing had really changed. I was still abusing drugs and off my psych meds. I was working at a restaurant and paying my rent and bills. I refused to believe that I had a mental illness that needed to be managed by medication. I didn't think that I had a substance abuse problem either.

That autumn I again began to experience psychotic thinking. Thoughts of angels and extraterrestrials in disguise as humans on Earth. Feeling immortal. Believing that I was on a special mission from God. Getting special messages from the TV and radio. Late one night, I thought I was being summoned by a divine force. I got into my car and first drove to a bad section of Pittsburgh. This is not somewhere you want to be in the middle of the day, let alone the middle of the night. It is rife with gang activity. I got out of my car and started shadowboxing. A couple of the homies just stared in amazement at me and let me do my thing. I thought that God was testing my faith to see how truly invincible I was. I then drove to a grocery store. I was so manic that I left my car unlocked and the motor running because God was testing my faith. I got some seltzer water off the shelf and proceeded to the checkout line. There was nobody manning the cash register. There was a police officer staring right at me. I thought that he was telepathically communicating with me because he was really an android created by extraterrestrials. I deduced that he was telling me that it was OK to walk out of the store without paying for the water. So I walked out without paying. The officer never said anything or stopped me. To this day I wonder how and why I got away with shoplifiting in front of a cop. Then I drove into downtown Pittsburgh. It was 3:00 in the morning. I got into town and retrieved a newspaper that had been delivered to a storefront. I saw a man on the street, walked up to him, and gave him the newspaper in a very official manner. He laughed and said, "Thank you." I then drove toward the Pittsburgh International Airport. I pulled over at an auto service garage. I got out of the car and etched my own form of hieroglyphics into the ground, as a curse on George H.W. Bush for killing innocent Iraqi people in the Persian Gulf War. I sprinkled the ground with the seltzer water. All of a sudden, these lights came on, and I was surrounded by a squad of police. They had this garage under surveillance because of recent robberies. When I saw that I was surrounded by law enforcement, my instincts told me to get on one knee, much like a kickoff returner in football signals for a touchback. The police asked me what I was doing there, and I told them that I had been "thinking too much." They asked me to drive my car back with them to the police station. They did not arrest me or put me in a cell. I was so manic. I thought this whole incident was a joke. They asked me for a family member's phone number to contact. I gave them my father's number. He came and escorted me back to his home. I really dodged a bullet during this experience.

My mother recognized my troubling behavior and convinced me to go to a drug rehab in the middle of Pennsylvania, about a 2 ½-hour drive east. I lasted there about a week. I didn't like the side effects of the medication they put me on – Stelazine. I checked myself out against medical advice. When I came back to my apartment, I did start to feel afraid of my thoughts and feelings – a lot of crying then followed by laughter.

Chapter Eight

It wasn't long before I wound up as an inpatient at St. Francis Hospital, then at a drug and alcohol rehab facility, then back at St. Francis Hospital. This was through the spring of 1993. The D & A rehab was a 28-day inpatient drug and alcohol program. I did benefit from the recovery skills I learned there. However, I would have been better suited on a Dual Diagnosis Unit. Dr. M.H., who was my psychiatrist, had me on lithium and Tegretol. There was a disconnect between him and the psychiatrist at rehab. As a result, my lithium level was not monitored very closely. The normal therapeutic blood serum level of lithium is between .8 and 1.2 mg/dL. By the time I was discharged from rehab after 4 weeks, my lithium level was at a toxic 4.5 mg/dL. During my inpatient stay, the side effects of the lithium were severe: extreme constipation, blurred vision, and tremors in my hand. Every 5 to 6 days, I would give birth to a constipated turd that was putrefying in my colon. I had been the ping pong champion, but lost that distinction because my blurred vision was so bad that when I was playing, I would see 3 ping pong balls coming back at me and didn't know which one to hit. When we participated in AA and NA meetings, we would gather and hold hands and recite the Lord's Prayer. I remember getting strange looks by the people I was holding hands with because my hand tremors were so acute. I tried explaining these side effects to the nursing staff, but they didn't take them seriously and kept dispensing the lithium. Plus the lithium and Tegretol did not seem to address my delusional thinking. After my discharge from rehab, I was committed to abstain from psychoactive substances. I attended local AA and NA meetings. However, I still needed inpatient psychiatric care. I was hospitalized back at St. Francis for approximately six weeks. During that time, Dr. M.H. decided to put me on Thorazine in addition to the lithium and discontinue the Tegretol. The medical residents were amazed that I was put on Thorazine because it was considered obsolete. Dr. M.H. explained to them that Thorazine was an old standby and quite effective.

I do remember not being able to sit out in the sun very long because Thorazine makes one's skin extremely sensitive to sunlight.

There was something quite magical about the television/smoking room on the mental health unit at St. Francis Hospital. Although the patients were not allowed to carry cigarette lighters, you would go into the lounge, ask a staff member for a light or, better yet, ask another patient for a light by taking the lit end of their cigarette and lighting yours with it. Then I would indulge in my delusional fantasias by interpreting special messages through the television or newspaper. Because I was in a hospital setting, I felt that my psychosis was somehow being validated, that I was truly on a special mission, not in the "nut house." My uncle the physician was pushing my mother for her to agree for me to have shock treatments, ECT (electroconvulsive therapy). My sister intervened and pleaded to my treatment team not to "fry my brain." After about 6 weeks in the hospital, I managed to come around and was discharged. I was now 26 and had managed to stay sober for almost a year. I even abstained from smoking pot and agreed to a psych med protocol. I had no source of income and found myself living with my mother and stepfather. The Thorazine made me sleep until 3:00 in the afternoon, but over time, Dr. M.H. discontinued it, and I was just taking the lithium.

For the first time in many years, I had found some stability in my life. I enjoyed my sobriety because I was staying clean for my Higher Power. I was even attending AA and NA meetings frequently – at least 2 per week.

One August evening in 1993, my sister and I went out to eat at a restaurant. There was a band playing, so we decided to stick around and listen to the music. Out in the parking lot I noticed a vanful of college-age kids who were having a good time. I surmised that they were probably smoking pot in the van. I excused myself from my sister's company and approached these kids. I asked them if I could smoke with them. They said sure. It had been about a year since I had smoked pot, and I enjoyed it. My tolerance was very low after being abstinent for so long. It only took a few puffs for me to get high. After that evening, I purchased some pot and began smoking on a daily basis. I was living on the third floor of my stepfather's house. Whenever I would smoke, I would make sure to close the door on my floor, stuff the bottom crack of the door with a towel, and I would smoke in the bathroom, blowing the smoke out the window. But my mother could still smell the distinct odor of marijuana. I enjoyed the ritual of smoking before going out on a run and getting into the music I was listening to.

Shortly thereafter I noticed that my mother had some Hycodan cough syrup in her medicine cabinet. I knew that Hycodan was a narcotic and it would get me high. I drank some but noticed that I did not experience the crush of the opiate rush or any sedating effects. I couldn't understand why I wasn't feeling anything. I decided that either the cough syrup was old and had lost its potency or the psych meds I was taking somehow acted as an antagonist to opiates. I made up my mind that quickly that I would stop taking my lithium to see if I could start feeling opiates again. Lithium is not a medication that you just want to stop taking abruptly without medical supervision. My body had grown accustomed to it, and it was controlling my psychotic thinking. I was so mad that I couldn't feel opiates anymore that I rationalized, "Nobody's going to take my rush away!" Of course, I didn't tell my psychiatrist that I had stopped taking my psych meds. I remember experiencing dizziness and lightheadedness the first couple weeks after I had discontinued my medication. But my theory was correct. There is something about psychiatric medication that nullifies the euphoria-producing effects of opiates. They are opiate antagonists.

My mother suffered from rheumatoid arthritis and always had a copious supply of Darvocet, which is a mild narcotic analgesic. After the lithium was out of my system, I pilfered some of my mother's pain medication. Lo and behold, I felt the euphoria produced by the Darvocet.

Even without my psych meds, I managed to stay relatively stable, while continuing to live with my mother and stepfather. I was continuing to eat healthy and exercise regularly. I was even working at a health food store. But I was smoking pot every day and raiding my mother's medicine cabinet quite frequently. I wrote Dr. M.H. a letter stating that I no longer needed his services.

By 1995, the dominoes began to fall one after the other. My thinking became psychotic. My mother realized this pretty quickly. One afternoon I walked to the local newsstand and shoplifted a magazine about UFO's. I thought that the aliens were testing me, and I had to prove my loyalty to them by stealing the magazine. The newsstand was owned by an elderly couple, and I stole right in front of them and walked out the door. I could hear them yelling at me, but kept walking. I thought that this was a true test of courage. Another time, I went to a coffee shop and hid a candy bar in my hat without paying. Another patron witnessed this and brought it to the attention of the owner. He kicked me out and warned me never to come back. These are examples of when mental illness is so severe that it causes criminal behavior. By that summer, my mother called the police and paramedics on me. They extracted me from the home and took me to the local hospital's mental health unit. I was an inpatient there for two weeks. I had tickets to see the Grateful Dead for a show at Three Rivers Stadium on June 30. My doctor was very sympathetic and discharged me on June 30. I remember attending the concert and even in my somewhat manic state, I realized that "the trip was over," at least for me. Jerry Garcia looked and sounded very ill. About a month later, I wound up back at the hospital. I started smoking cigarettes, since there was no pot to smoke. The second time I went back, the social worker had no sympathy for me this time. I remember him asking me, "Why don't you get off the drugs?" I recall feeling insulted by this question. Again, I didn't believe that I had a drug problem. Furthermore, I told him, "Because they make me feel good." I believed that marijuana and opiates were just as important to me as food and water. I was arrogant and thought that I was smarter than the doctors and my treatment team. I didn't think I needed psych meds. I didn't think

I was really mentally ill. These are classic symptoms of mental illness. I was scrambling like Roger Staubach or Terry Bradshaw because I knew that the psychiatrist and social worker were in control of my immediate future. I tried to do anything that would make me appear to be well, so that I could go home.

Chapter Nine

In August of 1995, the social worker from the hospital drew up the paperwork and had me committed to the state hospital. I was waiting to be transferred there, when I found out that Jerry Garcia had died. I didn't want to believe it and concluded that the announcement of his death was a hoax, like the rumors of Elvis and Jim Morrison's deaths being faked. My four-month stay at the state hospital is a saga in and of itself, but to summarize, it was truly a nightmare. I was prescribed Risperdal and Depakote. These meds made me gain 50 pounds in 4 months. It was a true stagnation of function, like being entombed in a mausoleum. No privacy. The confinement. Nothing to do all day but to attend an occasional group therapy, which I couldn't sit still for because I was overmedicated. Terrible food. No dignity and being in the company of people with severe mental health and mental retardation problems. One guy in group talked about abusing "Pepsihol," a combination of drinking Pepsi and rubbing alcohol. His driver's license had been revoked. Another guy injected the whisky Yukon Jack intravenously. Someone else shared his story of stealing a barrel of pesticide from a farmer. He and his buddies would bring it into their home, seal off all doors and windows, and open the barrel to get high off the fumes. He would also inject orange juice intravenously because the citric acid in the juice would get him high. Another poor soul discussed the fact that he had been at the state hospital for two years. This frightened me and was the motivation for me to elope. I eloped from the grounds for 12 hours but was summarily brought back by the state police in handcuffs. I had convinced a friend on the pay phone to come rescue me. He put me up in a hotel room about 45 miles away from the hospital. It is much more difficult to elope from the state hospital today, as all visitors must sign in with a guard and wear a visitor's badge. All patients now are required to wear a photo ID on the grounds. My elopement irritated my doctor, and she wound up adding another month to my stay. I recall a fellow patient asking me details of my escape. He was enamored by it. He asked me if it was worth it. I said yes because I got to enjoy a few beers and watch cable TV in a hotel room. Shortly after our conversation, I remember seeing him being put in seclusion.

As my disability attorney said, "The state hospital is no picnic." Ironically, for one afternoon it was. During the fall of 1995, the weather was still warm enough for the patients to enjoy an outdoor picnic. We had baked potatoes and hot dogs cooked on outdoor grills. The grounds sit on many acres of lush farm land. The leaves on the trees were beginning to turn colors. It was a beautiful sight. Often visitors would exclaim how peaceful and serene the grounds were. It's one thing to visit the state hospital and marvel at its intrinsic beauty. It's another thing to live there against your will. Nice scenery is the last thing on your mind to appreciate.

Patients could work their way up a level system. The lowest level was "SO" or "suicidal observation," where you were confined to the ward and under constant observation by staff. The next level was "escort," where you had limited freedom on the ward, but had to be escorted anywhere else in the building. The next level was "building," where you were allowed to travel freely within the building where you were housed, but not outside. The highest level was "grounds," where you had complete freedom to be inside the buildings or on the hospital's grounds.

Even with this ostensible freedom, all I wanted to do was lie in bed. I had four roommates, one of whom was this severely retarded fellow who looked like a cross between Nikita Khrushchev and Curly from the Three Stooges. At night he would yell, "Turn off TV! Turn off TV!" Patients were allowed to go to bed as early as 9:00 PM or as late as 11:00 PM. All of my roommates snored as loud as the MGM lion. Because the nightmare of being there was so profound, I always elected to go to bed as early as possible. It was my only solace and comfort. I could dream reality away. However, some patients were night owls and wanted to stay up and watch television as late as possible. Even during the day, I wanted to stay in bed. The staff frowned upon this. They finally moved me to my own room, which I thought was a promotion. The real reason was that this room had a lock on the door, so that staff could lock me out of my room during the day so I couldn't lie in bed. Some of the staff were more tolerant and would leave my door unlocked and didn't care if I lay in bed during the day.

My healthy eating regimen was secondary to just savoring the pleasure of eating anything. That's all you basically had at the state hospital: food and cigarettes. So I did partake in hot dogs and grilled American cheese sandwiches on Wonder bread. I drank 10% real juice fruit drink or milk. I did get permission with some resistance from the staff for visitors to bring me polar water. They wouldn't let me keep it in my room. I had to go to the nurses' station to ask for it. There was no access to clean, filtered water. I'm not talking from the tap, which contains pharmaceutical wastes, chlorine, fluoride, fecal matter, pipe sediment, and other toxic residues. However, most institutions, including hospitals, hospices, and assisted living facilities get their drinking water from the tap. This is a human atrocity. You can get plenty of soda pop, milk, and artificial beverages, but no good drinking water, unless you pay for it in bottles from a vending machine. When you're a patient at the state hospital, every quarter is precious to you. This is totally illogical. In fact some of the behemoth hospital organizations should install sophisticated water distilleries to make accessible clean drinking water to their patients.

I'll never forget the men's bathroom on the unit where I was housed. There were shower stalls, toilets, and sinks. But right in the middle of the bathroom, without any privacy whatsoever, was a bathtub. I remember thinking to myself, "Who would ever be inclined to sit in this tub and take a bath out in the open like this?" I called it Agamemnon's bathtub. Agamemnon was the commander-in-chief of the Greeks during the Trojan War. Upon his return home, he was slain in the bath by his cheating wife Clytemnestra. This institutional bathtub at the state hospital was a metaphor for how vulnerable and exposed I felt there.

I was discharged in December of 1995 one week before my 29th birthday. I lived in a community residence for a while. Then I moved to West Virginia to live with a buddy of mine and his girlfriend. They were very nice and accommodating to me, even though as my buddy Gary said, "You don't have a pot to piss in." I tried finding work at Kenny Rogers' Roasters and Taco Bell, but I was so overmedicated on the Depakote and Risperdal that I could barely function, let alone hold down a job. People told me that when they held a conversation with me, there would be a one or two-second delay before I would respond. The frightening thing is was that I was not aware of this social dysfunction. All I could think of during those brief attempts at work were, "I need to lie down and have a cigarette."

I recall the Pittsburgh Steelers being on a playoff run and eventually making it to the Super Bowl, which they lost to the Dallas Cowboys. All of my friends were so excited about this, but I was in such a disturbed state of consciousness, that it meant very little to me.

In February of 1996, I drove back to Pittsburgh to see if I could start my life over again. My mother wanted nothing to do with me, as was the case with my father. Luckily, my friend Kurt lent me $700, and I was able to secure an apartment. I got a job delivering pizzas and slowly got out of the pit I had fallen so deeply into. I started to see Dr. M.H. again. He commented that I had that "neuroleptic look" (heavily tranquilized) about me. I was torpid and had tobacco-stained fingers. Over the next year, I continued to take my psych meds, but was depressed over the 50 pounds I had gained. I smoked pot heavily. That was the only thing I looked forward to after a full day of pizza deliveries. I abstained from the opiates, as I knew that I would not feel their effect due to the psych meds.

I was buying my pot from a local character named Rico. He reminded me a lot of the character Squiggy from the 70's sitcom "Laverne and Shirley." He would say, "Hello, Phil? Phil? Hey, ah, what are you doing? Let me ask you something, would you be interested in a little high test?"

At the beginning of 1997, I once again, decided to discontinue my psych meds. I was disgusted with my weight gain and had decided that the only way to lose it was to stop taking my medicine. One fateful day in February, Rico called me up and told me he had my weed for me. He told me that he had something important to talk to me about. I drove up to his apartment. I saw my quarter ounce of reefer sitting on his kitchen table. Next to it were two lines of white powder. "Hey, ah, would you like to try a little high test?" The high test was his slang term for the synthetic form of heroin, known as fentanyl, the same substance I had snorted 6 years earlier in stamp bag form. Rico would get his in bulk, so he would just seal it up with the corner of a newspaper, so there were no wax bags with clever slogans on them. He called it the high test because he equated it to high-octane gasoline, as compared to the "balloon" which was the more standard grade of real heroin that was contained in a small plastic baggie and sealed inside a non-inflated balloon.

When I snorted the high test that fateful day, I remember the rush being instantaneous. All of those negative feelings and emotions from having been at the state hospital and feeling betrayed and abandoned by my parents were wiped away. The curtain of despair had been lifted. It was like a vacation from reality. The high test was a mental hiding place for me. For the next 6 weeks I went on a high-test festival. Interestingly, the buzz was so satisfying that I had no desire to smoke pot, which meant I no longer had that voracious appetite associated with marijuana. I immediately lost 25 pounds. I managed to get a hold of my addiction and concentrated on healthy eating, juicing organic produce, and running again. I lived near a cemetery and enjoyed running in this peaceful setting. I was also inspired to look for work in television. I got a job as a studio cameraman at a local Christian television station. I paid close attention to the testimonies and sermons of the preachers on our talk shows. I found it interesting that they would often claim to have conversations with God or were influenced by angels. In any other setting, they would stand a good chance of being involuntarily committed to a psychiatric hospital. But on Christian TV, this type of grandiose thinking was welcomed and encouraged. Things were looking up for me. By the summer I had lost pretty much all of the 50 pounds I had gained while at the state hospital. My abuse of the high test and the balloon came in waves. I would binge for a week or two, followed by complete abstinence for 10 days or so, only to look forward to my next binge. Of course, I made sure to pilfer plenty of my mother's Darvocet when I was coming off the high test, as without them the withdrawal would have been horrendous.

The other aspect of my health that I played close attention to was my digestion and elimination. Opiates insidiously undermine digestion. They dehydrate the body and slow down peristalsis, the natural muscular contractions the digestive system employs to move food from the esophagus to the stomach, small, and large intestine. Ultimately, abusing opiates can cause major constipation and gas. I remember, at times, feeling like I had the planet Jupiter in my stomach – a giant ball of gas. Being aware of this, I found a colon hydrotherapist who could work some real miracles on me after a heroin binge. The digestive system needs to be like the calm waters of the sea, not a tempest. Opiates hold your digestion hostage. The colon needs to be released from its bondage. As one of my science teachers once told me, "If an organism can't eliminate its waste, it dies." And that is the profound truth. Getting regular colonic irrigations during this time probably saved me from developing diverticulitis or irritable bowel syndrome or some kind of other serious organ damage. Looking back on this period of my life, it is so clear to me now that my addictive behavior truly mimicked that of someone with mania or bi-polar - from one extreme to the other. Chasing the opiate high at all costs, feeling the low of withdrawal and digestive problems, feeling high from cleansing the filth out of me, only to do it all over again.

By the spring of 1998, the heroin binges became more frequent and lasted longer, while the periods of sobriety and exercise diminished. I took unrestrained pleasure in it. I quit my job at the television station and lived off some disability settlement money that I received from social security. I started smoking cigarettes again and was a fixture in the local junkie scene. My IQ would plummet every time I would hang out with Rico. We would drive to really bad neighborhoods to score dope, and I always felt like I was on an adventure with him. Part of the heroin rush was just the procurement of it, without getting robbed, shot, or busted by the police. I began having manic thoughts and expressed lament to Rico over what happened to all the souls of the dinosaurs after the Ice Age. Rico acted as my therapist and said, "Maybe God shrunk them into iguanas!" I had seriously considered getting on the methadone program. The problem with that was that once you get on methadone, you're pretty much hooked for life. Just because it is a pharmaceutical drug and it is distributed by trained professionals makes it no less powerful than heroin. I had tried methadone a few times and found the high to be quite incredible and long-lasting. To have to take it every day seemed like that would only make me more dependent on opiates. I would have considered getting on methadone if I would be allowed to take it only 2 or 3 times per week. Rico's girlfriend was on it, and she claimed that it would make her joints ache and cracked most of her teeth. I knew that I could beat the high test, but it was just a matter of being so enthralled by feeling the initial rush after snorting it. By the summer of 1998, I was blowing all of my disability settlement money on heroin. As one of my friends put it, I was looking for synthetic love. At least 3 times per week I would have pretty much the same routine: drive up to the money access machine and withdraw $200. Just the smell of the new crisp $20 bills that were dispensed out of the MAC machine would make me dry heave, as I knew that soon that poison would be in my system. I would then drive over to Rico's apartment and pick him up. He would drop me off at my place, and then he would use my car to go get the high test. He always took a gun with him. I never knew where he went or who rode in my car with him. I just wanted to feel my rush. I can recall feeling mentally unstable and asking my psychiatrist for lithium. He was reluctant at first, because he was under the impression that I was taking Depakote and Risperdal. I had lied myself into a corner. He had no idea that I had stopped taking my medicine and was abusing heroin. My body was craving lithium, in an attempt to stabilize myself mentally. Dr. M.H. did give me a sample bottle of Eskalith. I would take one tablet daily and did feel myself stabilizing, but then I would abuse the heroin. This was a dangerous combination. It was the inspiration for the title of this book. I recall being on lithium and heroin that summer and getting really overheated. I literally would recline one foot away from a fan trying to enjoy my buzz, when really what I was doing was trying to convince myself that my version of self-medicating was safe and therapeutic. I briefly spent one week at St. Francis Hospital's Dual Diagnosis Unit in July. I had confessed to Dr. M. H. that I was hopelessly addicted, and he was obviously concerned about me. The hospital stay did not help me except keep me clean for 7 days. Within 2 days after being discharged, I was back to my old ways. In fact, one of the patients I met on the Dual Diagnosis Unit had been in the Navy. He persuaded me to spend some of my disability money on an escort service. I had never considered hiring a prostitute. Since I didn't have a girlfriend, and I longed for human companionship, I did indulge in his recommendation. Sex and drugs. That's what our culture endorses.

One night in August, as I was continuing my downward spiral, I noticed that I couldn't urinate after snorting 2 or 3 lines of the high test. I tried everything to pee, but I just couldn't relax my bladder enough to let the urine flow. I was concerned, but this didn't phase me enough to stop snorting more lines. By 3:00 in the morning, my abdomen started swelling below the navel, and I really had to urinate, but nothing would flow out of me. At this point I realized that I had a medical emergency. Luckily, the local hospital was within walking distance of my apartment. I figured that I would have to be catheterized and that they could get the urine to flow out of me. When I got to the emergency room, I told the staff that I had taken 2 Vicodin tablets and couldn't pee. They knew I was lying by just taking one look at me. The nurse did catheterize me, and I filled almost 3 colostomy bags full of urine. That was close to a gallon of urine that came out of me. I found out that not only do opiates cause constipation, but they can also interfere with the kidneys and the ability for the body to excrete urine. The doctor came in and talked to me about administering Narcan. I knew about Narcan – that it was an opiate antagonist given to people overdosing on heroin. The doctor was concerned that I would continue having urination problems if he didn't administer the Narcan. I was in such denial that I thought all they have to do is drain my bladder and I could go home and snort more heroin. I agreed to the Narcan. I did not know what I was in for. The nurse administered it to me in an IV line. Within a few seconds I felt this freight train wave of lightheadedness and difficulty breathing. It felt as if someone was trying to turn out the lights on me and snuff out my existence. It was like when Don Meredith would sing on Monday Night Football, "Turn out the lights. The party's over!" I was fighting as hard as I could to stay alive and conscious. I remember reaching out to the nurse for her to hold my hand. She had no sympathy for me. She just turned her back on me and said that I was going through anaphylactic shock. Anaphylaxis is an allergic reaction to things like the venom of a snake bite or bee sting or, in my case, a drug overdose. Blood pressure drops dramatically, which is what caused that feeling of thinking I was going to die. I had the epiphany that we enter this world alone and exit this world alone. After this life-changing experience, I figured the hospital was going to keep me there for observation at least for a day. They did not. They noted in my chart that I had "touched the face of God." They released me immediately with the instructions to "discontinue Vicodin." I received a bill from them for $760. At first I was arrogant and thought, "I'm not paying this. Screw them." Then I had a change of heart and realized, "Is your life worth $760, especially considering the thousands you spent on heroin?" I finally did pay that bill. The quest for the "opiate rush" rushed me to the hospital.

At this point in my life, I realized that I had almost killed myself from overdosing on heroin. I began to realize that my OCD rigid self-control wasn't working because I needed an outlet like heroin, which was totally out of control. I stayed abstinent from heroin and marijuana for the next six weeks. I used the rest of my disability money to secure an apartment in the town where my mother lived, since I had reconciled with her. It still took another 6 months, until March of 1999 when I quit heroin completely. After my ER experience, I would see Rico occasionally because I was still obsessed with feeling the rush of the high test. I would snort a small amount and then run to the toilet to see if I could pee. When I could, I would be relieved and then discipline myself not to snort another tiny line for another hour or so. This was complete idiocy. I just had a self-destructive wish and a strong desire to dance with death.

The reason addicts come back for more dope despite the consequences is because substances like heroin and cocaine penetrate the blood brain barrier. The blood brain barrier is a membrane of the blood vessels that filters out pathogens, bacteria, and viruses from entering the central nervous system. The central nervous system includes your brain and spinal cord. Thus, drugs like heroin, cocaine, alcohol, nicotine, and marijuana get into your brain and spinal cord and essentially pierce your soul. They infiltrate who you are. Even chocolate penetrates the BBB and creates "guilty pleasure." However there are natural, non-addictive substances that also penetrate the BBB. The supplements SAM-e, 5-HTP, and Kava Kava can cross the BBB and create a feeling of well-being, without harsh side-effects. Conversely, I have found that taking the amino acid L-Glutamine blocks and interferes with cannabinoid receptors in the brain. So you won't get high from smoking pot if you're supplementing with L-Glutamine. Keep in mind that as Dr. Gallagher points out, "Emotions embed themselves in the nervous system." So those feelings of guilt and shame and anger physically manifest themselves in the brain and spinal cord like those stubborn barnacles on the keel of a ship. I suggest that the reader purchase Dr. Martin Gallagher's book "Dr. Gallagher's Guide to 21st Century Medicine."

Chapter Ten

I had been off psych meds for 2 years now, so it was no surprise that I had a psychotic episode in May. I remember feeling extremely paranoid, anxious, and the delusion that I was John the Baptist. I wound up at St. Francis Hospital again. I admitted to Dr. M.H. that I had been off my meds for 2 years. He was not pleased. In fact, he told me that if I withheld the truth from him again, he would stop treating me. I went back on the Depakote and Risperdal. The problem with starting and stopping psychiatric medication is that there is a strong chance that the medication won't work as effectively, as compared to taking it regularly without interruption. I noticed that I began to suffer from akathisia from the Risperdal. Akathisia is a state of agitation and restlessness caused by antipsychotic medication. There are medicines to help alleviate this, namely Cogentin. I had been on Cogentin before, while on other psych meds. This gave me blurred vision. It seems quite illogical to take one drug to counter the side effects of another drug and start experiencing new side effects. However, the akathisia was so profound that all I could do is walk around like a caged lion and smoke cigarettes. I was so desperate for relief that I asked my mother if she could spare some Darvocet. She took pity on me and gave me some. The Darvocet definitely worked to calm me down. In fact, I told my psychiatrist that this mild narcotic worked better than the Cogentin, and he wrote me a prescription for one Darvocet every 12 hours. Needless to say, it wasn't long before I would amass the Darvocet, so that I could take 3 or 4 at one time to get blasted. I admitted this to him and he said, "You're not getting Darvocet from me anymore."

I started gaining weight again, but at least I was committed to staying off heroin. My stepfather had died in the fall of 1998, so I was dedicated to helping my mother and being a companion for her, since she was starting to suffer from depression about her loss. In the fall of 1999, my mother was so depressed that she wound up at a psychiatric clinic in

Pittsburgh. This triggered a manic response within me to stop taking my medication once again and pilfer all her Darvocet, while she was in the hospital. Needless to say, I wound up at St. Francis Hospital one more time, and Dr. M.H. tried me on a new medication, Zyprexa. This was my last inpatient hospitalization, just a couple months shy of my 33rd birthday. It is sad to note that St. Francis Hospital no longer exists. Their mental health facility was the best, in my opinion, when compared to some of the other inpatient mental health providers I had been treated by.

Over the next year and a half, I was reasonably stable, staying off opiates and out of the hospital. I was still smoking marijuana and cigarettes but managed to maintain a job delivering pizzas. In the summer of 2000, my mother broke her hip. I concentrated my energy on helping her and becoming a caregiver. The Zyprexa controlled my mental illness, but at a cost of my weight ballooning to 220 pounds. I was in size 42-inch waist pants. This depressed me, but I figured that someday – I wasn't sure how – I would get back to a more reasonable weight of 160 pounds and 34-inch waist pants.

In April 2001, I was involved in a car accident. A garbage truck hit me from behind. As the ambulance was taking me to the hospital, I remember thinking, "I'm going to sue the garbage company for $100,000, and I'm going to get a lifetime supply of Vicodin." Luckily, I had no broken bones or any neck or back damage, just some soreness that went away eventually. Unfortunately, I did not receive a penny from the garbage company for pain and suffering because I had the limited tort option on my car insurance. However, I did become the king of Vicodin. The hospital referred me to an osteopath who was very sympathetic to my pain and suffering. For the next 4 years I became hooked on Vicodin. Interestingly, because I was only on a small dose of Zyprexa – 5 mg – I could feel the euphoria producing effects of the Vicodin without foolishly discontinuing the Zyprexa. Vicodin is a semisynthetic opiod made from hydrococdone bitartrate and acetaminophen. Although not as strong as heroin, the Vicodin helped me cope with seeing my mother suffer in intensive care and be confined to a wheelchair in an assisted living facility. And I had no problems urinating.

Vicodin maintenance became my own version of a methadone-type program. I didn't always take it every day, but it satisfied my opiate cravings. I remember for my 35th birthday, in December of 2001, I started the day off by taking 4 Vicodin and watching Teletubbies. As I felt the crush of the opiate rush, I was blissful when I saw the baby's head inside the sun. I thought all was well with the world. I concluded that opiates sure do take care of the moment. However, I was not ready to accept that they also rob you of your ambition.

In March 2002, I got a job as a portrait photographer at the local mall. This was truly rewarding work – taking pictures of infants, toddlers, high school graduates, and families. It was stressful work but very satisfying. Often, a grandmother or mother would say to me at the end of a particularly difficult sitting, "I bet you go home for a stiff drink after this." I had to bite my tongue from saying, "No, lady, I go home to two and a half extra-strength Vicodin." From Halloween until Christmas, the work was non-stop. I could photograph 10 families in a 5 or 6-hour shift. That is how I could develop and hone my skills as a portrait photographer. Family after family, kind of like on an assembly line. I looked forward to coming home to my Vicodin, especially during the holiday season. However, it definitely made me hung over the next day. It put me in a fog and robbed me of my quick wittedness. I would be hard-pressed to remember family members' names to instruct them how to pose.

In June 2003, I decided that I had had enough of weighing 220 pounds and wearing size 42 pants. I determined that the only way to get back to 160 pounds was to discontinue taking my Zyprexa. This was a costly mistake. I thought that I could fight my mental illness with my intellect and nutritional supplements. The weight did start coming off, but the psychotic thinking returned. I thought that my manager at work was a witch and that the assistant manager was from Jupiter. My behavior became very erratic, and I was fired from my job at the portrait studio in August 2003. I was devastated. It was like breaking up with a girlfriend. At this time, I grew increasingly paranoid. I thought that the cruise control on my car was connected to Dick Cheney's pacemaker. I thought that every time I would hit the accelerate button, Mr. Cheney would experience rapid heart beat and that a team of doctors was huddled over him in some bomb shelter trying to figure out what to do. I was convinced that there were government agents combing American cities looking to abduct healthy males in order to harvest their organs for elected officials. I remember not being able to sleep, as if I had drunk a pot of coffee before bed. I could doze off for a few minutes and then wake up in a hypervigilant state. I made a deal with myself, "Whatever you do, no matter how tempted you are, don't ever stop taking your psych meds again!" I had tried and failed too many times when I discontinued the meds. I got scared and asked Dr. M.H. for help. He increased my Zyprexa to 12.5 mg. This started helping me, but the increased dosage nullified my feeling the Vicodin. So, I started hopelessly popping more Vicodin just to feel even a tiny rush. Now I was running out of Vicodin before it was time for the next refill. I figured that my osteopath was going to get mad at me. Much to my surprise, he was very sympathetic. He prescribed me Duragesic for "opiod tolerant patients." Duragesic is a fentanyl transdermal patch. Basically, I was now using pharmaceutical- grade high test, but I could urinate with this stuff. He also prescribed me Xanax for anxiety and one Vicodin every 12 hours for "breakthrough pain." Duragesic is very expensive - about $700 per month. So I moved out of my apartment and used my rent money to pay for the Duragesic. I moved into my mother's house, as she lay dying in intensive care. My mother finally died in December of 2003. That was a rough time for me. I was now smoking marijuana and cigarettes like a chimney and back to being a varsity addict.

By February of 2004, I could no longer afford the Duragesic. I went back to the Vicodin, taking six tablets per day, plus the Xanax. I was caught in a rut, living in my deceased stepfather and mother's home, trying to have some semblance of a life. I decided to decrease my Zyprexa dose back to 5mg so that I could at least start feeling the Vicodin. I had a rough few weeks, but it worked. However, I was still taking up to six tablets of Vicodin per day and not every 4 to 6 hours as prescribed. I would wake up and take 2 tablets and then 2 hours later take 2 more and then 3 hours later take 2 more. By the fall of 2004, all of the Vicodin started to take a toll on my digestive system. I noticed that I would get these urges to burp but couldn't. I had this trapped gas sensation. And it always happened right after ingesting Vicodin. This alarmed me. I got together with my priest, and we started jogging together in the mornings. I cut out the cigarettes and started slowly coming out of the depression caused by my mother's death. I had about one month sober from the Vicodin on my 38th birthday in December of 2004. I decided to reward myself with 2 Vicodin, and again the burping problem returned. I was now convinced that I had to stop taking the Vicodin completely. I also wound up in the emergency room because I had taken some nutritional supplements that got caught in my throat. They wouldn't go down no matter how much water I drank. When the nurse took my blood pressure, it was 155 over 105. I knew instinctively that it was the marijuana that had raised my blood pressure. I began to decrease my pot smoking substantially.

I continued running and eating healthy again. I wasn't losing any weight, though, because of the Zyprexa. In February 2005, I took Vicodin and all opiates for the last time. This time the burping problem was really bad. It lasted for 10 days. I knew that the Vicodin was damaging my upper digestive system. At this time I had also approached Dr. M.H. about trying a different psych med that would control my illness but would allow me to lose weight. He suggested Geodon. I was now committed to no opiates, exercise, healthy eating, and sparing marijuana use. I had been taking the Geodon for about 10 days, when on March 6, 2005, my life changed forever. I was in church, when I noticed that the burping problem returned with a vengeance. This trapped gas sensation was constant. I couldn't escape it. No matter how hard I tried to burp, I couldn't. My body also broke out into a rash. I saw a gastroenterologist who indicated that he thought that I had a hiatal hernia also known as GERD (gastroesophageal reflux disease). He wanted to put a scope down my esophagus to confirm, but I was afraid of the anesthesia making the burping symptoms worse. Can you imagine? An addict turning down the opportunity to be sedated? He indicated that there was a new procedure where the patient swallows an endoscopic pillcam that takes pictures of the digestive system and transmits them to a computer. No anesthesia. No invasiveness.

I opted for that. Sure enough, the gastroenterologist's diagnosis was correct. I had Grade 2 GERD and Barrett's Esophagus (acid damage in the esophagus). A hiatal hernia occurs when the hiatus, a muscle which connects the stomach to the diaphragm, gets stretched or weakened, allowing the stomach to push up into the diaphragm. This also creates malfunctions with the esophagus and cardiac sphincter, which controls hydrochloric acid flow.

Although I had stopped taking the Vicodin, the damage had been done. I believe that the Geodon was the knockout punch. I discontinued the Geodon and went back on Zyprexa. The next year and a half was a nightmare of epic proportions. I experienced perpetual torment with my burping reflex. I actually contemplated suicide. I started smoking cigarettes again. I was furious with myself for allowing my addiction to create a permanent health problem. I was also mad at myself for trying the Geodon. I asked my psychiatrist if he thought I needed to be hospitalized. He said no and suggested I take the anti-obsessive medication Celexa. I was afraid to, given that the Geodon had aggravated my hiatal hernia. I also stopped smoking marijuana completely because it just made me obsess and panic more about my stomach. I no longer enjoyed the reefer buzz. Dr. M.H. pointed out to me that it was my anxiety disorder and OCD which were making the symptoms of my hiatal hernia seem worse than they really were. He assured me that my condition would improve. The gut is sometimes referred to as "the second brain." 70% of our serotonin and melatonin are manufactured in the gut. In fact, the gut has its own nervous system called the enteric nervous system. When your gut is not right, neither is your mind.

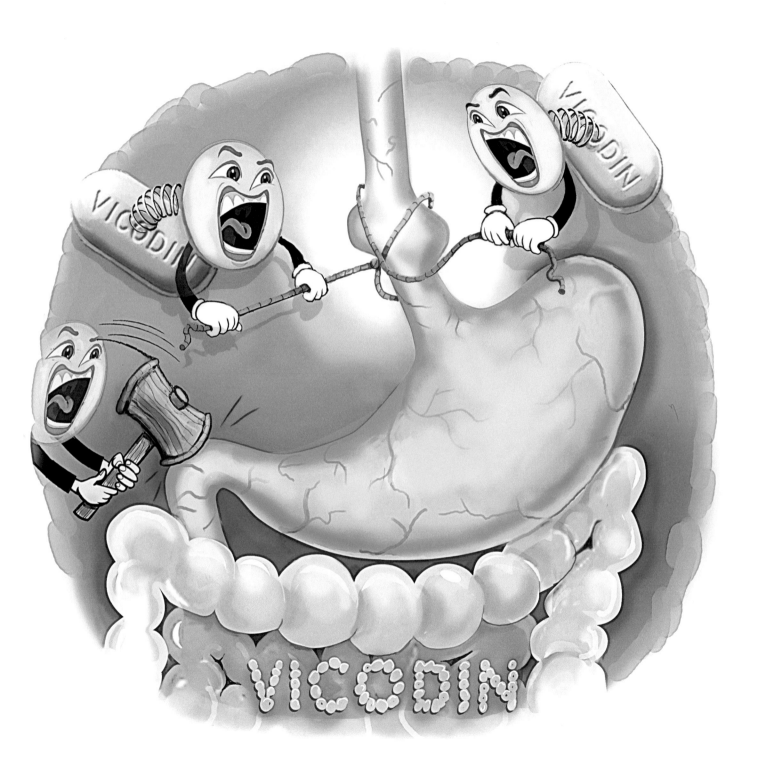

Chapter Eleven

In November of 2005, I began working for a mental health organization. At this time I also quit smoking cigarettes. It was good having a job to take the focus off my stomach. The burping reflex started to come back, and by October of 2006, I was pretty much able to burp whenever I had to. This syndrome was still abnormal in that I had constant, frequent urges to burp, especially after eating, but at least I could burp. The gas was no longer trapped. That sensation was what drove me to suicidal ideations. I was also thankful that I experienced no heartburn, as some GERD patients suffer from. Around this time I noticed that I could not eat large amounts of food at one time. I would feel full quickly after only eating a few bites of food. This is another common symptom associated with GERD. If I ate portions that I normally used to eat, I would run the risk of feeling bloated and pressure right below my sternum. One extra bite of a hamburger could make me sick for days. As a result, I became extremely disciplined when I ate. Only eating a few bites, then waiting 10 or 15 minutes, eating a little bit more, and so on. After eating this way for a month, I noticed that my weight started to drop, despite taking the Zyprexa.

By the summer of 2007, I had dropped about 40 pounds and was in size 36 pants. I continued to exercise regularly and eat healthy. Things were looking up for me. Over the next two years, I dropped another 20 pounds and was wearing size 33 pants. I got down to 148 pounds. My psychiatrist exclaimed that I was the thinnest person he knew that was taking Zyprexa. I managed to keep the weight off until early 2010. The weight started creeping back up, despite no changes to my medication, diet, and exercise routine. This was very frustrating. I shared with my doctor that the Zyprexa was like a cockroach. It adapted to my Spartan lifestyle and put the weight back on me. My psychiatrist corrected me and said that it was my body somehow that was adapting to the medication. I consulted with an endocrinologist, who determined that I do not have diabetes or even prediabetes.

Many anti-psychotic meds can cause diabetes because they increase insulin resistance. The body converts sugar into fat, instead of using it for energy. I also consulted with an integrative physician who tested my cortisol levels. Cortisol is a stress hormone released by the adrenal glands. When cortisol levels are high, men have a tendency to put on belly fat. I had read that when people are engaged in a vigorous exercise routine, the body can release high amounts of cortisol. I don't believe that I was overexercising. My routine worked for me, and I felt great. I think that a combination of middle age, hormone imbalances, and the Zyprexa contributed to me gaining all the weight back that I had lost. Yes, it's frustrating. But I don't let it get me down. I try to reflect that "we are all expanding with the Cosmos. Sometimes we have moments of contraction." Discontinuing the Zyprexa is not an option for me. I have been burned too many times before, after quitting my medication.

As Dr. James Winer points out in his radio programs, in the United States, we are 4% of the world's population, and we are consuming 75% of the world's drugs. Yet we are 72nd in overall health. That means that there are 71 other countries ahead of us that are healthier. If the Western, drug-consuming medical model were so successful, shouldn't we be in the top five? We run to medical doctors to get prescriptions for drugs to treat diseases that are mostly the result of the consequences of our lifestyles. We irradiate the food we consume in microwave ovens. The water we drink has pharmaceutical residues and other toxins like chlorine and fluoride, which can disrupt thyroid function. We don't eat enough fruits and vegetables, choosing man-made processed carbohydrates and artificial hydrogenated fats, instead. Is it any wonder that we are a sick nation? Cancer, heart disease, and diabetes are often the result of poor lifestyle choices. Dr. Gallagher points out that depression and anxiety can be attributed to nutritional deficiencies, food allergies, and accumulation of toxic metals in the brain. B vitamin and omega-3 fat deficiencies can cause depression. Allergies to wheat, dairy, and soy can cause anxiety even several days after consuming them. Our environment is polluted. So is our food. Mercury, lead, aluminum, and other toxic metals can cross the blood/brain barrier and embed themselves in our brain and spinal cord.

Dr. Gallagher points out that the next time you marvel at a beautiful snow scene on the ground and in the trees, keep in mind that every one of those snowflakes is contaminated with mercury.

I still eat healthy. I insist on an organic diet, meaning foods that have not been raised with toxic pesticides, herbicides, fungicides, steroids, or antibiotics. I'm "manic about organic!" I'll eat organic meat and fish at most 2 to 3 times per week. I'm big on juicing. I use my Champion juicer at least 5 times per week. One day I'll juice vegetables. The next day, I'll juice fruits. There's nothing quite like starting the day off by juicing organic carrots, beets, celery, kale, lettuce, and apples. Because the juice has been separated from the fiber, it is pre-digested and goes right into the bloodstream. This is nutrient-dense food and helps to alkalize the body. An overly acidic body is the root of many diseases, such as cancer and arthritis. I remember Jay, the Juiceman Kordich touting that drinking carrot juice is like giving yourself a blood transfusion because the constituents of carrot juice are similar to those found in human blood. Plus fresh fruit and vegetable juices bathe the brain in nutrients. When I juice fruits, I include pineapple and grapefruit or strawberries. I stock up on cranberries, when they are in season. Juicing cranberries is a great way to keep the kidneys and uro-genital canal healthy. Some people are opposed to juicing because of the lack of fiber and the high natural sugar content. I still eat fruits and vegetables to get fiber, but the juicing is a great adjunct to get one's recommended serving of 6 to 8 fruits and vegetables per day. I have been juicing for 25 years and do not have high blood sugar.

I only drink distilled water, nothing from the tap. Tap water is polluted with pharmaceutical residues and waste. Some experts claim that drinking distilled water is bad because it has no electrical charge and is devoid of minerals. This can acidify the body. I remineralize the distilled water I drink with concentrated minerals from the Utah Great Salt Lake inland sea bed. One quarter teaspoon of ConcenTrace Trace Mineral Drops remineralizes an entire gallon of distilled water. I abstain from coffee, which can raise blood pressure and is acidic. I do not drink soda pop, which really undermines health. The carbonic and phosphoric acids leech minerals from the bones. The high fructose corn syrup can contribute to diabetes. I also avoid genetically modified foods. GMO's are foods that have been genetically altered. For example, the DNA or genetic material of one organism is transferred to that of another. Splicing glyphosate in the toxic pesticide Round Up with a seed of corn in the hopes of producing better crop yields is perverted science.

I supplement daily with omega-3 fish oil, flax seed oil, stress B vitamins, and vitamin C. As Dr. Gallagher points out on his radio program, we've all heard of the cardiovascular system. But what about the cerebrovascular system? In other words, blood flow to the brain. The carotid arteries on either side of the neck feed blood to our brains. However, there are tiny capillaries on the brain that can easily get choked or congested with protein wastes called beta-amyloids. In autopsies of Alzheimer's and dementia patients, their brains are found to be loaded with these plaques and wastes. It has been found that omega-3 fish and flax oils can help reduce this concentration of waste in the blood vessels of the brain. Once or twice a week, I'll eat a raw clove of garlic and chase it with some honey. This bolsters the immune system. I focus my diet on fresh fruits and vegetables, nuts, seeds, beans, and whole grains. It's interesting to note that the eating disorder I had as a teen metamorphosed into a healthy eating regimen as an adult. I knew at a young age that what we put into our bodies was important, but I just didn't have the knowledge or experience to implement a healthy eating lifestyle. The aging process is all about what we put into our bodies.

There is a term called "orthorexia nervosa." It is not anorexia or bulimia. It is an obsession with eating foods that one considers healthy. I would consider myself orthorexic, but it does not make my life unmanageable. If I'm at a social function, and I know that the food may not live up to my normal standards, no problem. I will partake.

As Dr. Winer often states on his radio program, "We dig our graves with our teeth." If you're eating a healthy diet, your cells can replicate themselves without much degradation. But if you're living off junk food, the cells don't have the essential building blocks to reproduce themselves properly. It's like making a xerox copy on a machine. If you start off with a poor original and after so many generations of copies, you will eventually not be able to read the document, because the information has degraded.

Chapter Twelve

Not a day goes by that I don't live with the regret of having permanently damaged my stomach from drugs, but as in the Twelve Step Program of Alcoholics Anonymous and Narcotics Anonymous, "We admit to ourselves that we had become powerless over our addiction." I was truly powerless over my quest for the opiate rush. It took literally making myself sick to my stomach to finally stop.

You might ask me, "Phil, do you ever get the craving to take some Vicodin again, just to feel the rush?" The answer is no. I ingested enough opiates for the next 5 lifetimes. I know that even if I were to take half a Vicodin tablet, my burping reflex would become retarded again. I never want to experience that trapped gas sensation ever again in my life. In 2010, I fractured my left foot while jogging. This was very painful. I went to an urgent care center. They took X-rays and confirmed that I had fractured my fifth metatarsal. They dressed my foot and sent me home with a bottle of Vicodin. I followed up with my podiatrist, who also offered me a prescription for Vicodin. I declined. Then the urgent care center called me with the name of an osteopath to see. I told them I was under the care of my podiatrist. I share this because the old Phil would have used this opportunity to doctor shop and procure an arsenal of narcotics. In fact, the day I walked out of urgent care in crutches and receiving all the attention, I noticed some people in the waiting room whom I perceived as addicts. I was their wet dream. They looked upon me with envy. My biggest concern was, "How quickly can I heal so that I can start running again?" Some ice and elevation were my remedy for this injury. It did hurt for 2 weeks, but I was able to manage. I refused to take over the counter pain meds, as well, because I felt the risk was too great at aggravating my hiatal hernia. And you know what? My foot healed beautifully. I was back running within 10 weeks. I have no pain or discomfort. Sometimes the tendon around the metatarsal will twitch or spasm, but this occurs very infrequently. That bottle of Vicodin is still sitting in my kitchen cupboard six years later, sealed and unopened. It is my reminder that "one is too many and a thousand not enough," as stated in AA and NA.

Chapter Thirteen

I recently lost two close friends to suicide. My friend Reggie took his life in the Fall of 2011 at the age of 45. Reg and I had known each other since sixth grade. He struggled with mania and depression since his early college years. We stayed in touch after high school and regularly got together and talked on the telephone. He never had issues with substance abuse. But he could never find a medication that would control his manic highs. Unfortunately, some people do not respond to psychiatric medication and suffer from "medication-resistant depression." Reggie was one of those poor souls, although he fought a courageous battle. The last time I spoke with him, he told me that his treatment team had said, "There is nothing more that we can do for you."

My friend Sheila committed suicide in 2012 at the age of 29. Like me, she suffered from anxiety and depression since she was a child. She had been hospitalized numerous times, and our friendship was based on sharing coping tools for recovery. She was a pleasant person. However, life became too overwhelming for her.

As my priest points out often in his sermons, we should all keep in mind that we are eternal beings. The time we spend here on Earth is just a blip on the screen when compared to eternity.

In conclusion, it took 16 years for me to realize that self-medicating with narcotics was not the way to lead a productive and fruitful life. In other words, feeling good for 20 minutes during the initial opiate rush was not equivalent to the next three days of dysphoria after being hungover, going through withdrawal, and feeling guilty for using. Addicts have a selective memory and only think of the good times associated with using. We conveniently forget or block out 95% of the time of hell associated with using. We are constantly chasing a feeling of well-being, which diminishes over time, and the new high is not feeling sick or avoiding the physical symptoms of withdrawal. Now we get high just to feel normal and be able to make it through the day without feeling like we have the flu. Abusing narcotics is like borrowing from the future. We want to feel twice as good than normal now, when we get high. However, the consequence is feeling half as good as normal tomorrow when we are hungover and our neurotransmitters are depleted. I used to rationalize that when I would engage in an opiate binge, it was OK because it was like taking a rest stop, while traveling on the turnpike. The only problem with that analogy is that you become marooned at the rest stop and never continue back on your journey.

There are medications besides powerful methadone to help opiate addicts get back control of their lives. There is suboxone, which is a partial agonist, meaning that it may cause feelings of euphoria, but really helps control opiate cravings. It is a narcotic. However, Vivitrol is non-narcotic and blocks the opiate receptors in the brain. It is a monthly injection, and even if you were to take narcotics on Vivitrol, you would not feel their effects. Most importantly, it really controls opiate cravings and has been successful in controlling cravings for other substances like cocaine and methamphetamine.

Our nation is in the grips of an opiate epidemic. My story is not unique. People of all ages are finding access to heroin that is potent and cheap. Some may have been prescribed narcotic pain meds for legitimate pain and then become addicted. When their physicians will no longer prescribe, they turn to heroin, which is more economical than buying pain pills on the street. Because of the Good Samaritan Laws recently enacted, friends can administer Narcan to someone who is overdosing and be immune from criminal prosecution. Most opiate overdoses involve respiratory arrest, where the user turns blue from lack of oxygen. However, this is not the only way to overdose, as illustrated by my personal experience with kidney and bladder failure.

Chapter Fourteen

The work I do now for a local mental health organization is very rewarding. I have been with the agency since 2005. It is the longest tenured job I've had, namely because I am compliant with my psych meds and am opiate-free. I am an ombudsman, which means that I assist individuals who are on Medical Assistance navigate the complaint and grievance process pertaining to their mental health services. Being that I know what it is like to be mentally ill, I am usually able to identify when someone is experiencing a mental health crisis. I am also trained in Mental Health First Aid and recently became accredited as a Certified Recovery Specialist. A CRS is a peer for those recovering from addiction. One important formula I learned during the CRS training is "Abstinence + Change = Recovery."

A mental health consumer can come to the ombudsman and express their dissatisfaction to me. They may feel intimidated by their psychiatrist. There may be a cultural barrier with their doctor, if the psychiatrist is from a foreign country. The consumer may feel they are not getting the help or attention they need from their mental health casemanager or resource coordinator. The consumer always has the right to find the best quality of care they need.

Parents of children who receive mental health services often have to navigate the grievance process. A grievance occurs when the MCO (managed care organization) denies or decreases services for the child. Or a different service altogether may be approved for the child, which was not recommended by the evaluator/prescriber. The ombudsman assists parents file a grievance and provide testimony during grievance hearings to prove medical necessity to the medical assistance insurance company (MCO) for services such as BHRS.

Had I been born 30 years later, I probably would have benefitted from BHRS (Behavioral Health Rehabilitation Services), also know as Wraparound. A Behavioral Specialist Consultant (BSC) develops a treatment plan for home and school to help the struggling child or adolescent stay on task and reduce negative behaviors. The Therapeutic Staff Support (TSS) and Mobile Therapist (MT) implement the treatment plan. There are other mental health outpatient services for struggling families, such as Family-Based, Multi-Systemic Therapy (MST), and Targeted Mobile Therapy. In Pennsylvania, even if the parents have resources which would make them ineligible for Medical Assistance, the state qualifies the child for MA under the PH-95 loophole category. All other states require an institutional level of care, and most other states count income and assets of the child.

There is an epidemic of autism, ADD, ADHD, Asperger Syndrome, ODD (oppositional defiance disorder), juvenile diabetes, juvenile rheumatoid arthritis and other behavioral and physical health problems with children these days. Without getting into a heated debate or losing my credibility with the reader, I believe that vaccines are a major contributor to these emotional and physical disturbances in children. Recently, an Italian court ruled that vaccines do contribute to autism. A whistleblower from the Centers for Disease Control admitted that the CDC has been suppressing this information for years. For further information about becoming informed on whether or not to vaccinate yourself or child, I would suggest you listen to Dr. James Winer and Dr. Martin Gallagher on WKHB, 620 AM in the Pittsburgh area. You can stream these health programs around the world on khbradio.com. Keep in mind that these health shows are broadcast from 8 AM to 7 PM EST.

ΕΓΚΡΑΤΕΙΑ + ΑΛΛΑΓΗ = ΑΝΑΚΤΗΣΗ

ABSTINENCE + CHANGE = RECOVERY

84

Afterword

My friend Les has often said that tragedy plus time equals comedy. Mental illness and addiction are nothing to laugh at. However, now that I have been opiate and tobacco-free for over ten years and have not been hospitalized in over 15 years, I can look back and find some humor in my personal struggles. The illustrations that accompany this book are not meant to ridicule, but rather to satirize my odyssey and recovery from dual diagnosis. Guilt is worrying about the past. Fear is worrying about the future. The key to joyful living is to be content for the moment, without panic or worry and the subsequent need to self-medicate.

About the Author

Phillip Graph lives in Pennsylvania. He has been in recovery from mental illness and addiction since 2005. He currently works for a local mental health organization. His last psychiatric hospitalization was in 1999, and he has stayed well by taking the medication Zyprexa and abstaining from opiates. He regularly shares his recovery story at local colleges, universities, and mental health facilities. His message is that dual diagnosis is not an irrevocable fate and can be overcome. Mr. Graph enjoys running, photography, and filmmaking.

Printed in the United States
By Bookmasters